CASTANEDA

FOR BEGINNERS™

ILLUSTRATED BY MARTIN ARVILLO

BY MARTIN BROUSSALIS

Writers and Readers Publishing, Inc.
P.O. Box 461, Village Station
New York, NY 10014

Writers and Readers Limited
35 Britannia Row
London N1 8QH
Tel: 0171 226 3377
Fax: 0171 359 1454
e-mail: begin@writersandreaders.com

Spanish Edition:
Castaneda para Principiantes,
published by ERA NACIENTE SLR
Arce 287
Buenos Aires (1426)
Argentina

First Published by Writers and Readers 1999
Text Copyright © 1998 Era Naciente SLR.
Translated by Latin Words - John Brookesmith

A Writers and Readers Documentary Comic Book
Copyright © 1998
ISBN # 0-86316-281-9
1 2 3 4 5 6 7 8 9 0

Printed in Finland by WSOY

Beginners Documentary Comic Books are published by Writers and Readers Publishing, Inc. Its trademark, consisting of the words "For Beginners, Writers and Readers Documentary Comic Books" and the Writers and Readers logo, is registered in the U. S. Patent and Trademark Office and in other countries.

Writers and Readers

publishing FOR BEGINNERS™ books continuously since 1975

1975:Cuba • 1976: Marx • 1977: Lenin • 1978: Nuclear Power • 1979: Einstein • Freud • 1980: Mao • Trotsky • 1981: Capitalism • 1982: Darwin • Economics • French Revolution • Marx's Kapital • Food • Ecology • 1983: DNA • Ireland • 1984: London • Peace • Medicine • Orwell • Reagan • Nicaragua • Black History • 1985: Marx's Diary • 1986: Zen • Psychiatry • Reich • Socialism • Computers • Brecht • Elvis • 1988: Architecture • Sex • JFK • Virginia Woolf • 1990: Nietzsche • Plato • Malcolm X • Judaism • 1991: WWII • Erotica • African History • 1992: Philosophy • • Rainforests • Miles Davis • Islam • Pan Africanism • 1993: Black Women • Arabs and Israel • 1994: Babies • Foucault • Heidegger • Hemingway • Classical Music • 1995: Jazz • Jewish Holocaust • Health Care • Domestic Violence • Sartre • United Nations • Black Holocaust • Black Panthers • Martial Arts • History of Clowns • 1996: Opera • Biology • Saussure • UNICEF • Kierkegaard • Addiction & Recovery • I Ching • Buddha • Derrida • Chomsky • McLuhan • Jung • 1997: Lacan • Shakespeare • Structuralism • Che • 1998:Fanon • Adler • Marilyn • Postmodernism • Cinema

contents

questions 1

beginnings 2

migration 3

life in america 4

peace & love 5

the streets of san francisco 6

drugs 7

writers of the time 8

rebellion & renewal 9

primary interests 10

conflict 11

...encouragement 13

notes on knowledge 14

herbs, cacti & mushrooms 15

a powerbase 17

peyote 18

first lessons 20

toloache 21

smoke 24

flying 25

allies 26

a special state 27

the first book 30

the power of protest 31

reviews 32

a path to follow 33

return journey 34

learning to see 35

controlling confusion 37

death 38

more teachings 42

suspending interior dialogue 44

stopping the world 50

expansion of consciousness 51

personal history 52

changes 54

sleeping	55
friendships	56
attitudes	57
cigarettes	58
other habits	59
self importance	60
but what is to be believed	61
the hunter	62
grievances and doubts	63
secrets of the hunter	64
not worrying	65
breaking the routine	66
the way forward	67
games	68
the art of participating in dreams	72
what has become of me? what shall I do?	74
a riddle	77
a firefly	78
the luminous seed	80
centre of the self	81
the two rings	83
a challenge	83
an encounter with power	84
the mystery of the world	86
the tonal	87
the nagual	88
the sorcerer's explanations	92
farewell	94
the leap forward	95
form & patter	97
love	101
sex	102
empty spaces	103
the toltics	104
what are the true aims of the toltec?	105
the eagle	107
the task	111
joe cordoba	115
shrewdness & survival	118

writing	121
advanced consciousness	123
readers of the infinite	125
silent knowledge	126
the centre of decisions	128
the adversary	129
pragmatism & spirituality	132
without words	133
the ongoing group	134
how many are there?	135
more studies	136
three kinds of attention	137
the first kind of attention	138
the second kind of attention	139
the third kind of attention	140
intention	141
being conscious of being	143
the assemblage point	144
the two bands	148
stalking	149
principles	150
precepts	151
more on the art of dreaming	152
the double	153
the ancient shamans	154
the new seers	155
don juan's lineage	154
castaneda's legacy	157
shuttin the gates	160
business	163
philosophy	164
from magical passes...	165
...to tensegrity	166
final attainments	167
a happy memory	168
castaneda's terminology	169
the authors	171
index	172

The life of **Carlos César Salvador Arana Castañeda** — to give him his full name — is full of notes and anecdotes, which are sometimes contradictory. Who was this man whom people have so often tried to categorise?

He was probably unique among those contemporary authors who have coined the most new meanings of words and phrases ...

... and many more. A single mention of any of those terms can call up not only the writer himself but his books and his master — **Don Juan**.

Now, thirty years after his rise to fame and following his recent death, he is still important, as are the books he wrote and the stories that have been spun around him. But what sort of a life did he lead?

beginnings

Largely because he decided, purposely, to erase his personal history, there is little consistency in the facts and circumstances of Casteneda's life. But this is what we are given to understand:
– it seems he was born on December 26, 1926 in Cajamarca, Peru. But he himself said he was born in Juquery, a village near São Paulo, Brazil, on the same day in the same month, but in 1935. Other sources give different dates and places of birth.
He started school in Cajamarca and later left with his family for

Lima, Peru. There he undertook further education by studying painting and sculpture at the National School of Fine Art.

However, Castaneda maintained that he was sent to a boarding school in Buenos Aires, Argentina, and that later he went to Italy to study art in Milan.

In any case, from an early age he took up arts and crafts (his father was a goldsmith) and he went on making drawings, paintings and sculptures until the end of the 50s. He considered the possibility of making a living as an artist and he had also started writing.

Castaneda said he had a very difficult life. Very early he showed signs of living every moment to the full and breaking all ties and commitments.

Records show that at the age of 15, Castaneda went to the United States, arriving in San Francisco in 1951. He graduated from Hollywood High School, living with an adopted family, then from 1955-9 he followed various courses at the City College of Los Angeles. He studied creative writing, journalism and psychology.

During those years he survived by driving taxis, selling ponchos, working as a petrol pump attendant, barber and tailor. He also became assistant to a psychoanalyst. There are hundreds of tapes recordings of those sessions.

> *In essence human conflicts have much in common.*

In 1959, he acquired US citizenship, dropping his father's name, Arana, and taking his mother's name, Castaneda, with no accent on the 'ñ'. He enrolled at UCLA and three years later took a degree in anthropology, Until 1971 he maintained a link with the University. Since that time he regarded English as his working language, in which all his books were written.

For me, a way of life is not introspection nor mystical transcendence but being present in this world.

In 1960 he was married, in Mexico, to Margaret Ryan, an American woman some years older than himself. They lived together for only a few months but were not divorced until 1973. His son, Carlton, was born in 1961.

At the beginning of the sixties, a pacifist movement among young people was taking shape, and the hippies rose to prominence. Their movement was to become known as flower power. Their idealism, opposed to the lifestyle until then considered as 'normal', along with their interest in drugs, promoted a new way of thinking, feeling and loving.

Then were sown the seeds of the struggle against the power of the establishment and for the power of the people in general and of black people in particular.

As the restrictive McCarthy era drew to a close, the younger and less satisfied elements in society were gathering in force.

In the Age of Aquarius. the gathering together of people became important, in living, in loving and in the celebration of the new music, rock. Work was frowned upon and war was seen as by far the worst activity. American intervention in Vietnam was about to escalate.

In that city, at that time, a certain social phenomenon made itself apparent. With certain Californian colleges and university campuses in its region, San Francisco was like a magnet to people looking for a freer life. In legendary districts like the Haight-Ashbury, old houses could be rented at moderate prices, with few questions asked. The city was full of jazz and rock musicians. The major influences, some of them still to be felt today, would be **The Grateful Dead, Jefferson Airplane, Jimi Hendrix, Janis Joplin, Santana, Joan Baez** and **Bob Dylan**. Some of the protest element in folk music was merging with rock. And then there was **Frank Zappa**. Also, some African musicians came to settle in California, bringing their particular percussion instruments and style of performance. Because of **The Beatles** and their interest in oriental culture, from religion and philosophy to clothing and lifestyle, there would be those from India too, particularly **Ravi Shankar**, giving concerts and letting people properly appreciate the sitar, the tabla and other sounds.

Not everything is peace and love in this movement ...

You don't think so?

Frequent use and experiments with certain drugs held a powerful place in the movement — LSD was most important to the hippies. The famous guru of the trips, suddenly possible with this hallucinogenic substance, was **Dr Timothy Leary** (1920-97. In 1960 he was holding seminars on psychedelic drugs with his students at Harvard and so he was later dismissed from his post. He stated that an individual's capacity for creative thought and imagination was limited only by a personal inhibition upon dreaming.

The writer **Ken Kesey** (b. 1935), author of **One Flew Over the Cuckoo's Nest**, used to travel in a very special bus, experiencing the journey through antonomasia — finding new names for things.

Toward the end of the sixties, LSD became a classified drug.

Dr Thomas S. Szasz (b.1920) suggested that coca, marijuana, psychedelic mushrooms and poppies are plants which, along with their by-products, take immediate and beneficial effect without danger, having been so used since time immemorial. Marijuana and opium, as analgesics and sedatives. Coca, to allay certain symptoms. Peyote, to induce extraordinary experiences. These substances had always been at people's disposal, showing that to prescribe medicines for oneself, as to choose one's own diet, must be among the most elemental of human rights.

Why this special social and political interest in drug use in the twentieth century?

It was the era of the Beat Generation. Jack Kerouac (1922-69), author of *On the Road*, and Allen Ginsberg, (1922-97), author of *Howl*, were among the most notable, along with Gregory Corso (b. 1930) and the poet and publisher Lawrence Ferlinghetti (b. 1919). William Burroughs (1914-97) was to write *The Naked Lunch* and tell of his experiments with narcotics.

Many books that young people were reading at that time were of seminal importance, such as *The Doors of Perception* and *Heaven and Hell* by Aldous Huxley (1894-1963) and *The Lord of the Rings* by J.R.R. Tolkien (1892-1973). Alan Watts (1915-73) brought some major principles of oriental philosophy to the fore, essentially with his *Way of Zen*.

In search of new experience and illumination, people were beginning to travel to Mexico, Paris, Tangier and India. Within the United States, communications among hippies developed rapidly from coast to coast.

In the summer of 1960, the works of Henry Miller could at last be published in his own country. Not only his *Tropics* would have a great effect, but notably *Big Sur and the Oranges of Hieronymus Bosch* would be taken up by the hippies and many others also, taking up residence both in those 'gardens of delights', camping out in Miller's garden and around Big Sur on the California coast.

Now I don't know what more I can do!

... neither do we.

This reaction against hierarchies, against western religion and conformism reclaimed the right to enjoyment of the senses, with no conventional restraints. Sex became unshackled, in all its practices — the limits lying only within the reach of each individual's imagination. By 1967, the movement had gained in popularity almost worldwide, particularly in cities like London, Amsterdam and Paris, and spreading as far as Buenos Aires.

Yet a few years later the flame had been extinguished; although almost all of the music and the poetry lived on, developing further, to make those arts what they are today. Without idealising it, it does have to be said that the movement did highlight new varieties of creative activity and opportunities to make free choices. The questioning of values, considered until then unchangeable, affected most of all those ways of life stemming from bourgeois morality and sexual repression: the balances of power between men and women, parents and their offspring, lecturers and students. Beyond the immediate results, paths were opened up to point forward to other prospects for living.

primary interests

In the summer of 1960, as an anthropology student, Castaneda travelled to the south-eastern United States to research the medicinal plants used by the Native Americans of the region. Dr Meighan, his ethnography tutor in California, promised an 'A' grade to those who managed to interview any Amerindians. Thus advised, Castaneda gathered together some interesting material along the way. With an eye on publication, he thought of amplifying his CV by writing a concise essay on his findings. His aim was to enrol as a postgraduate so as to become a university lecturer.

One day he was waiting for a bus in Nogales – a Mexican frontier town – to go back to Los Angeles. A friend was with him, following the same investigations ...

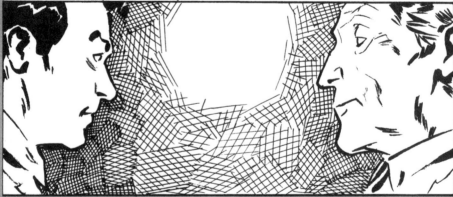

The friend attempted some introductions and Castaneda tried to make an impression upon an acquaintance that he did not yet have. He thought that way he could gain the Indian's confidence, but the man stared back at Castaneda without saying anything. The student felt stupid, but he was still driven by his own curiosity.

conflict

The Indian was a sorcerer, a wise man, a shaman who had been initiated into the ancient wisdom of the Yaqui and the Yuma, of the Toltec nation. His name was Don Juan Matus.

Still entrenched in his university background, Castaneda visited Don Juan at his home in Sonora, Mexico, over a twelve-month period. He felt confident the data he was to obtain would put him in favour with the university faculty, and so he could gain some advance in the teaching profession. At that time, Castaneda was the classic Hispanic immigrant with allegiance to the United States. He was steeped in a particular ideology of development: knowledge, which leads to power, can be seen to be validated and legitimised in an academic environment. He set much store by this undertaking. His thought processes followed a classical line of reasoning, basic to western logical thought and the European cultural tradition. His scientific method evaluated everything in terms of proof, verification and explicatory theory.

Castaneda and Don Juan became friends, but as yet there was no mention of peyote. Castaneda was a long way from identifying the true interests of the sorcerer. He was not aware that Don Juan would transmit to him a series of precepts, and that a trap would have to be set to lure him on. They spent long hours together.

The years that passed from 1960 to 1973, recorded in Castaneda's books, were very significant: he would learn another way to lead his life and to perceive reality. And that would be very different from the way he had previously known ...

11

The sorcerer would suggest to Castaneda another pattern of knowledge, founded not upon the relations of cause and effect, but upon the wisdom of a millenary tradition with its own principles of logic and signification. It was based on the forces of energy present in every living thing. Also different was the method of apprenticeship, which required enormous effort from the novice. Don Juan subjected Castaneda to some almost cruel tricks, arduous treks across the desert and the flatlands, hunting expeditions, encounters with things unknown and with forces unforeseen ...

Castaneda found himself in a perpetual dilemma, pulled on one side by his intellectual skepticism and on the other immersed in a world beyond his control, which was escaping him and which little by little would transform him.

Don Juan afforded access to his own system of sensory interpretation. It was equivalent to a new process of social imprinting, in which new practices were to be learned for interpreting perceptual data. In that context, Castaneda was at the outset an outsider, without the means to construe intelligently the messages of magic. This forced him to reappraise his principles.

For the Native American, the phenomenon generally known as magic has for thousands of years been a serious and authentic practice, comparable to science. Don Juan was not concerned whether or not his propositions would be taken seriously by Castaneda. He elucidated his arguments, despite his apprentice's opposition or incredulity or failure to understand. It is characteristic of shamanic instruction that diverse subjects are discussed in a relaxed or natural manner, without following a prearranged pattern or structure.

notes on knowledge

Eventually, after one year, Don Juan explained to Castaneda that he had acquired the knowledge of a shaman from another sorcerer, having been led through a kind of apprenticeship.

The shaman is a man of wisdom, he who knows.

> I am going to teach you the secrets of a wise man ... You will learn to your own cost, that is the way it is.

> I take notes only to remember. Gathering pages together gives me a sense of balance and purpose.

Castaneda — who was forbidden to take photographs or to record any tapes — took notes constantly, even in the most unexpected places and situations. Initially the sorcerer tried to prevent him, then he made light of it and in the end he encouraged Castaneda to write.

He used all the notes he had taken in putting together his first book.

herbs, cacti & mushrooms

In order to teach and formulate his knowledge, Don Juan used three psychotropic plants:

- TOLOACHE (Datura inoxia)

- PEYOTE (Lopophora Williamsii)

- HONGO (Psylobice mexicana)

Long before the Europeans came, Native Americans had known of the medicinal and therapeutic properties of these plants. In ritual and magical practices, they were used to induce, physiologically, states of ecstasy and spiritual illumination.

Similarly to meditation and asceticism, the use of drugs had become a physical and intellectual discipline within this ritual context. Inner freedom, vision and wisdom could thus be found.

There are many kinds of hallucination. The most common are visual, usually colourful, but certain plants can affect different senses, in mysterious and inexplicable ways.

The sorcerer referred to these plants and mushrooms as vehicles to take a person toward forces and powers beyond the self. The states of mind so produced could lead to the mastery of such forces and powers.

Castaneda saw this special kind of perception as separate reality, as opposed to the reality of everyday life. On the other hand, Don Juan considered these states of mind to be not extraordinary but as concrete aspects of everyday life.

Psychotropic plants contain chemical substances capable of inspiring psychic processes.

For the shaman, these states of mind are realand not mere hallucinations.

a powerbase

Before initiating him into the secrets of mescalin, as the active ingredient of peyote is known, the sorcerer put Castaneda to the test: he had to find his powerbase. That is to say, the place where he could most suitably discover his energy.

After six hours ...

How am I doing, Don Juan?

Almost close your eyes!

... so that he could find that energy.

peyote

Some weeks later, Don Juan and Castaneda went with some other Indians to a house where mescal buttons (the dried tops of the peyote) could be found. This was Castaneda's first experience with this hallucinogen. The sorcerer had described it as a benevolent protector with a mastery over humankind and a power of its own. Mescalin could have a connection with wisdom. If peyote accepts the person who seeks it, it appears as a human being or as a light. It will give up its secrets only little by little, showing the way to a better life, even though that may be horrendous when first encountered.

Castaneda chewed on his mescal buttons ...

I FEEL MY VISION IS CHANGING

Peyote is seen as a deity by the Indians of the south-western United States and in the north of Mexico. The next time that Castaneda used it, he was taking part in a special four-day festival, called a *mitote*. At a *mitote*, shamans join together to develop model ways to live life correctly.

So Castaneda met with **Mescalito**, the spirit of mescalin.

Don Juan spoke of the enemies of knowledge.

First: fear, in the face of which there should be no drawing back. Then, heightened awareness can show how not to slip back into bein impetuous, being a clown. Having achieved this, one has to learn how to use these new powers. Finally, not to give way to the desire give way to the decline of old age.

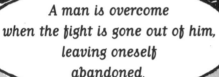

A man is overcome when the fight is gone out of him, leaving oneself abandoned.

Knowledge has to be approached as if going to war: wide awake and cautious but absolutely confident.

toloache

This is known as the devil's herb. A variety of it, another dangerous member of the *datura* family, is known in English as thornapple. The sorcerer showed Castaneda how to prepare it. It is linked to the acquisition of power. It depends on the use of a male plant, together with a female one. They have to be dug up very carefully, using a branch from a greenwood tree. Every part of the plant has a special function. The root is important for the conquest of power. The stem has healing powers. The flowers can effect personality changes and the seeds strengthen the brain. The technique of preparing oils and distillations from toloache and all the rituals that go with it come from a far distant past.

Castaneda drank the liquor and also used the ointment produced from the plant.

The devil's herb serves many purposes. For seeing, for travelling hundreds of kilometres.

The herb is only one way among hundreds of ways. Anything is just one way among hundreds of ways.

If you feel you should not go that way, under no condition go there. You have to lead a life of discipline to keep clear.

Look closely and test it out as often as you feel you need to. Then put forward a question.

Does this way lead to the heart of the matter?

No way leads anywhere. Some ways have a matter at the heart of them, others do not.

How do I know if I go wrong?
Perhaps, at the time, the way that does not lead to the heart is comfortable and that might suit me.

Foolishness!

A WAY WITH NO HEART TO IT IS NEVER PROFITABLE.
ON THE OTHER HAND, A WAY THAT HAS A HEART TO IT COULD BE EASY:
YOU DON'T HAVE TO WORK HARD JUST TO BEGIN TO FOLLOW IT.

smoke

Castaneda tried a mushroom, called smoke or smokey.

This one too relates to the acquisition of power. At the end of each year, several ingredients are collected, prepared and stored. The mushroom is dried and ground and left for a year. Then it is mixed with five other dried plants. The mixture is a personal one.

The pipe and its trappings are objects of power. When the sorcerer passes on from this world, he will pass the pipe on to his disciple.

This mixture is for smoking with a pipe.

On one occasion, when smoking, the sorcerer showed Castaneda how to turn himself into a crow. For this, it is important to learn certain eye movements, crossing them. This makes the eyes see two separate images. Allowing two different arrangements of things to be seen, this technique prepares one to understand that more than one world is possible.

In the first two years of Castaneda's apprenticeship, the sorcerer used the word *allies* to mean toloache and mushrooms: the ways they could be used. They are forces, neither good nor evil, which shamans use to point out a direction. Because of their spiritual qualities, they can be fabulous guides and guardians. They attract the emotions. And they have no given shape. Their appearance changes for whomsoever may see them.

Don Juan confronted Castaneda with these guardians. Sometimes the apprentice felt he would go mad with fear.

26

In September 1965, Castaneda recorded that he had experienced a **special state of** **separate reality**. This time it was not the result of hallucinations, but of careful manipulation by the sorcerer ...

Somebody caught your soul to kill you or make you seriously ill.

While I investigate, remain at your powerbase.

With your soul you won the battle. When someone has clear and strong intentions, feelings are no obstacle.

Now what happens, Don Juan?

The sorcerer surprised Castaneda yet again — half trickster, half friend. He openly rejected the areas of traditional knowledge of which Castaneda had been so proud. Don Juan set him down in front of situations which had frightened him all his life. The sorcerer was applying a rigorous practice of instruction. Meanwhile Castaneda gained in strength and power.

Last night you learned many things. We live in a predatory world, full of life-or-death challenges.

The art of the sorcerers

the first book

Harold Garfinkel, founder of Ethnomethodology, and one of Castaneda's departmental supervisors, persuaded him to improve the manuscript of his first book, **The Teachings of Don Juan – a Yaki Way of Knowledge.** Castaneda rewrote it three times. It was published in the USA in 1968 and earned the author his master's degree.

1968 was a legendary year in Europe and America. A student movement sprang up in Paris in May. Respect for authority was crumbling. The uprising was to apply critical force to the traditional university structure. It attacked segregation, teaching methods and materials, as well as the distance and dogmatism of the faculty. It also united the students in their opposition to consumer society.

They took to the streets and set up barricades to confront the Paris police. **Daniel Cohn-Bendit (Danny the Red)**, figurehead of the movement, was held for questioning, which had the effect of holding the various student groups together. Trade Unions came onto the scene. The economy came to a halt and social unrest spread throughout France.

The Unions laid claim to new rights. The students, who were looking for revolution, set free a wave of ideas under the slogan **PROHIBITION FORBIDDEN**.

They were prevented, as **J.-P. Sartre** (1905-80) had pointed out, by the absence of a leader with a full political agenda. But the questions they had raised were a breath of fresh air, showing that the cards could be reshuffled and dealt again.

the power of protest

During the '60s black people's struggle for civil rights had grown and had become organised as a potentially powerful opposition in the United States. In Detroit and Chicago this opposition was severely resisted. In 1968, following the assassination of Martin Luther King and during the Democratic Convention in Chicago, there were serious riots in both northern cities – not only against racial and socioeconomic discrimination, but against the increasingly political power of the Chicago police. Images of black people's demonstrations and counter-resistance were televised and seen around the world.

In that same year of 1968 there was student rebellion in 37 countries. That was the social climate of the time: particularly in Berkeley, California, where students had already been protesting against the Vietnam War for some years. More serious opposition was emerging among students and young people in what was then West Germany. In the Netherlands the Provo and Kabouter movements emerged, challenging the economics and the values of classic bourgeois society. In Spain, the power of General Franco was more openly contested that ever before. In October '68, an uprising of Mexican students was brutally suppressed.

But for the Mexican writer **Octavio Paz** (1914-98), the message of the uprising, *worldwide*, had been above all a moral one. Young people were living out ideas and ideals which had been put forward immediately before the time when the student rebellions occurred. By the first years of the '70s, their revolution and their criticism had almost died away.

reviews

With his first book, Castaneda was launched as a publishing success and became a cult figure. He also caused a stir in academic and intellectual circles, as well as among those going against the current. Hundreds went into the Mexican desert, looking for Don Juan, while many drug users saw him as a kind of patron saint.

There were some who saw Castaneda as a literary figure of psychological and spiritual importance. Others saw him as a dissenting intellectual who was shifting the grounds for academic investigation and instruction.

There were also those who saw Castaneda as an impostor, a dealer in legends and fables. These were the ones who required proof of the existence of Don Juan and who rejected the book. They criticised Castaneda for lack of objectivity and pointed out some contradictions.

Nevertheless, his work and his image continued to attract attention. For so many people, the things he had to tell had come to occupy a very important place in their lives.

Castaneda gave talks in bookshops and universities, but he was saying things that still provoked hostility among some people. They felt he was a danger because he spoke of destroying certain patterns of behaviour.

While people around him were making their different opinions heard, Castaneda was modifying and applying the teachings of the sorcerer to his own life. Then it was that he began to erase his own personal history. He would not allow himself to be photographed nor his voice to be recorded.

From that time on, a stream of anecdotes began to circulate about his personality, which fed and reinforced the legend.

At the end of 1965, Castaneda had suspended his apprenticeship to the sorcerer, weakened by the participation and commitment required of him. But in April 1968, with a copy of his book in his hand, he felt compelled to show it to Don Juan.

Over a meal, Castaneda observed some street children and expressed some pity for them.

To see is a special way of perceiving, enabling one to arrive at the true nature of things. It is to perceive energy as it flows through the universe.

What is seeing, Don Juan?

Where is the turning point, the vantage point?

You have to learn that for yourself ...
seeing is not looking.

You are able to distinguish one thing from another. You know how to appreciate things as they really are, as for example seeing a person as a luminous seed.

In this sense, the warrior's path is a continuous manoeuvre, conceived as support for other warriors, so they can directly reach their target — perceiving energy.

Seeing is not the same for everybody.

Everything is as new, when it is seen, and the world seems unbelievable.

We learn to think of all things as we train our eyes to look at all things, while we are thinking. Our actions seem important because we have learned to think that they are.

controlling confusion

A person who sees can control confusion and has no active interest in those around him, because seeing disengages him from everything he has ever known.

death

Don Juan referred frequently to death, although his remarks were meant more to throw life itself into relief, rather than to prepare for a life beyond.

For the shaman, life is at the service of death. Awareness of death is a way to purify present actions.

Don Juan told Castaneda that he thought of death with no remorse nor pain nor concern.

Concentrate on whatever lies outside of time ... so that every action is your last battle on this earth.

If not, your actions will be those of a frightened man.

In the face of death, there is no time for trivialities. Being conscious of death, one has the courage to transcend death's limitations. This attitude does not allow for gestures of doubt nor remorse nor frustration. Rather, this attitude favours actions of true surrender.

Death is the only wise counsellor we have.
Ask for that counsel when you feel annihilated.

Death will tell you that nothing really counts ...
Death will tell you 'still I have not touched you'.

One day, Don Juan took Castaneda to see his friend Don Genaro, at Oaxaca, in central Mexico. This man, also a sorcerer, was of the Mazatec people.

Whilst conversation was characteristic of Don Juan's teaching method, Don Genaro used a highly creative physical display. He could travel many kilometres in an instant: he would shift at once from an open space to a distant mountain. In this way he sought to abolish Castaneda's logical reasoning, defying the classical laws of time and space.

They went out walking, until they reached a great waterfall.

Suddenly ...

?!

Genaro wishes to help you to see, but you are very inhibited.

Therefore the sorcerer made Castaneda smoke a few more times, despite the unease and fear this caused him. He did not want to repeat those experiences. But the shaman was unwavering in his intentions. He showed Castaneda that he knew nothing of the forces he had touched upon, and reminded him that a warrior is never in another's hands, stopped dead in his tracks, waiting for a hail of stones. Thus he could reduce to the minimum the hazards of the unforeseen. While he was smoking, a peasant appeared before him ...

What happened?

You are learning to see. That takes time and effort.

A warrior puts everything to the test, without anxiety. He alone has the power of his decisions and he is the master of his choices. Once a choice is made, there is no time for regret or recrimination.

So fortify your life strategically.

So, it is a way of free will. One day you achieve the impossible. A power is arising ...

He could touch anything, with the aid of a sensation that came along the umbilical cord: that is willpower. Then it could be said that a warrior is a magician, a shaman, a sorcerer.

The sorcerer warned Castaneda against talking too much within himself. The world is of a determinate form because we tell ourselves it is. If we cease from repeating this definition to ourselves, the world ceases to have that form. To arrive at the opposite of interior dialogue — that is to say, interior silence — implies an enormous revolution. On the one hand lies the world: life, death, humankind, relationships, everything that surrounds us. On the other hand lie the things that human beings have made and done, which lend comfort and security. They may be very important, but only in certain measure and in a certain sense.

A warrior does not set store by anything that renders humankind greater than the world itself. And he treats the world as an interminable mystery, and the things that human beings do as endless confusion.

Castaneda was much altered, having searched — entirely alone — for his 'ally', fulfilling another challenge that the sorcerer had posed to him.

Go home and do not return until you have recovered.

Castaneda benefited from working for several months on the notes he had taken. At the same time his hopes of ever understanding the wisdom of Don Juan were diminishing. In October 1970, he was writing the final pages of his second book, **A Separate Reality** (1971).

One phase had ended and another was about to begin ..

When Carlos Castaneda returned to Mexico, he met again with Don Juan and Don Genaro.

He could hear an extraordinary reverberation, followed by a noise even stronger. Then he could see.

After ten years of apprenticeship, Castaneda could no longer subscribe to his old conventional standards for determining reality. Faced with the ways of Don Juan and Don Genaro, his mind found itself at a dead end. At one level, he could comprehend the new perceptions and sensations the two wise men had offered him. But on another plane he was still resistant, still looking for rational explanations.

I thought that seeing the world through using drugs was the only way to learn the teachings of Don Juan ...

... but it isn't like that!

In May 1973, Castaneda again travelled to Sonora to see Don Juan.

That was the origin of his third book, **Journey to Ixtlán** (1972). With that he was awarded a doctorate.

But another great surprise was on the way.
The basic precept of magic is that reality, or the world we have all come to know, is only a description ... just one among many.

All things that come into contact with a child function as though a master were describing those things and their world to the child; until such time as the child is able to perceive the world according to its description.

In the flux of interpretations which becomes perception, almost never does the configuration of the world appear under scrutiny.

stopping the world

To be able to see, it is necessary to stop the world. That means one has to cease to observe it in the form — until now never doubted — that it is given by the process of socialisation. To do this changes everyday life because it halts the course of interpretation. Things are appreciated in a different manner, in accordance with a different description: that of sorcery ...

Castaneda revised once again all his notes, to cover that technique and to include it in his book.

expansion of consciousness

Psychotropic plants and mushrooms are not essential (although in some cases they are useful) for the description of the world according to magic. There are other means and occasions which also act upon the personality, expanding consciousness. Castaneda realised that most of the experiences the sorcerer exposed him to were techniques for deconstructing his consciousness. The means and intensity of the use of drugs must depend on the receptivity of the apprentice to knowledge. Some people do not need them. Don Juan gave drugs to Castaneda because of his difficulty in breaking with cycles of routine. This was impeding him in grasping a new description of the world. The plants and mushrooms enabled him to establish his own **point of leverage.**

You are very stubborn and you do things clumsily.

Do you want to break with old attachments or don't you?

The sorcerer showed him the importance of leaving personal history behind. First of all, he had to wish to do so. Then he had to cut off from it little by little. Don Juan explained that personal history could be inconvenient.

Castaneda would have had to renew that constantly, recounting to his friends and family all that he was doing. If he broke with the past, he would not have to give any reasons. Nobody would be offended nor disillusioned by his actions.

Nobody can shackle you with their own thoughts.

Thus you can put a smoke screen around yourself.

We can take things as gospel — or not. This can be exciting and can keep us on our toes, without us having to behave as if we knew everything.

The sorcerer persuaded Castaneda to change his habitual perceptions. He found himself at a crossroads. He could not return to his previous way of living, of seeing the world ... but nor had he acquired enough new knowledge to act upon. Nevertheless — since the time his first book had appeared — he had begun to change many old habits. Above all, he had adopted the notion of concealing himself. Henceforward he would obliterate perfectly his personal history.

Concealing oneself does not mean disappearing altogether. It means being in complete control of one's involvement in events, among people, making one's own choices.

Castaneda gave up reading so much: he read the **National Enquirer**, almost exclusively!

From the copious correspondence he received, he would select a

Perhaps I'll reply to this letter.

letter at random: that would be the one he would read.

Thus he fulfilled another of the sorcerer's teachings: to be inaccessible to most people and to make himself accessible to power.

Castaneda's time for sleeping and dreaming amounted to five hours in all, divided into night time and daytime slots. This sleeping pattern necessitated being able to fall at once into a deep sleep.

The sorcerer advised him not to take a rest if he felt upset. If upset, it would be best to sleep in an armchair.

We have been taught to go to bed and to get up at regular hours because that is what society requires of us.

friendships

The sorcerer was adamant in saying that keeping up friendships with those with whom one had nothing in common would be a sure way to lose energy.

One day Castaneda made a call to his home in Los Angeles. The house was, as always, full of people. He asked a friend to find a suitcase that had some of his things in it.

Where shall I bring it for you?

I'm in hospital.

Keep the books, the records and all the rest.

Castaneda's friends thought he had lost his mind. They gathered all his things together, as if they were on loan to them. Then they waited to see what would happen.

Castaneda, who was about to move into a small apartment, did not meet up with his friends for another twelve years, when he thanked them for their friendship and so brought another episode of his life to an end.

This dispels obsession.

Castaneda was learning not to lose his grip. The shaman taught him that a warrior must behave as if he were always in control, even when he might be shaking with fear.

Thanks to the influence of Don Juan, Castaneda changed his attitude towards love and sex. He terminated a relationship that had been full of conflict. He arranged to meet the woman in a restaurant. While they were eating, the usual thing happened: they had a row. She shouted at him, insulting him.

Do you have money?

Yes.

Let me go to the car for a moment.

He decided never to see her again.

cigarettes

The sorcerer told Castaneda to bring a supply of cigarettes, because they would be spending a few days in the hinterland of Chihuahua. Castaneda, who was a chain smoker, put them in his rucksack.

One morning ...

Where are my precious packs of cigarettes?

A coyote made off with them.

There you could buy cigarettes.

For one whole day they tried to track the animal down ... but it was not to be found. Nor did they find the village which Don Juan had insisted was nearby.

Days went by and they were not yet able to make the descent from the high plateau.

When the moment arrived, the sorcerer found he could discover the way back down. So, after ten or twelve days, Castaneda had given up smoking.

I'm lost ...
I'm getting old ...

other habits

Castaneda also changed his diet. Once, Don Juan pointed out that Castaneda often seemed unwell. He finally admitted it. Then he took to eating only one kind of food at a time. Several times a day, pausing often, he ate only a few mouthfuls.

According to Toltec dietary custom, a mixture of foods is bad for the health. They say that the habit of mixing different foods has developed quite recently in human history, and that to eat only one staple food aids digestion and is better for the system.

A regular pattern in daily life is best and any change of pattern can cause an adverse effect throughout one's being. We are tied down by many habits. The traditional direction of 'not doing' is precisely opposed to the regular routine to which we are accustomed by society. In this way, all manner of new avenues may lie open.

All the faculties and possibilities of sorcery are to be found within the human body itself.

self importance

In the course of his teaching, the shaman singled out Castaneda's self importance as something he should be prepared to lose. Don Juan taxed him with disguising complacency as independence, saying that his self importance was effectively a hindrance to caring for himself. Castaneda had to remodel his behaviour so as to be able to learn.

Sometimes Castaneda would feel for a moment that the sorcerer was a dangerous person out of control. Also he would not stop looking for a rational explanation for every unusual situation to which the Mexican was exposing him. But at the same time he had a profound attachment to Don Juan.

Think before making a decision, and afterwards forget yourself: there will always be a million decisions waiting for you to make. Now go and chop some wood. That will calm you down.

let's hope that's possible

61

Don Juan was also training Castaneda to become a hunter. Castaneda had apparently had some hunting experiences as a child, already. To be a hunter means to know many things and to be in perfect balance with everything around oneself.

One day, while checking some traps ...

Do you think that you and I are equals?

Of course.

No, I am a hunter and a warrior and you are a sitting duck.

grievances and doubts

The sorcerer said that Castaneda did not plan his own battles but only those of strangers ... that he was not interested in learning about plants, about hunting nor about anything at all ... that the world of the sorcerer was infinitely more useful than the idleness of Castaneda's life.
Afterwards he remained motionless for several hours. Castaneda realised that Don Juan was capable of staying like that forever if need be ... and that his world was indeed superior. He also took account of the fact that for himself, Castaneda, and for many others, the real problem is a personal state of extraordinary slothfulness, which people elevate to some concept of personal freedom, so that nobody else may bother them.

For the shaman, the secret of the great hunters consisted in being within reach and out of reach, in the proper following of the track.

A hunter is inaccessible because he does not constrain nor disturb his territory. He enters upon it lightly, taking from it whatever he needs and then he quickly vanishes, almost without trace.

To worry is to put oneself within reach, without wishing to do so. A person who worries will desperately grasp at anything, as if grasping at straws, and so becomes exhausted. In that way he loses and exhausts the thing or the person that is being hunted.

> *Do not worry.*
> *A hunter knows*
> *he can attract game*
> *to his traps*
> *over and over again.*

breaking the routine

Don Juan often insisted that Castaneda should change the routines of his earlier life. Those old ways can make people predictable or make them prey to others. The hunter's purpose is to make sure he is never the prey. Paradoxically, the priests of ancient Mexico encouraged the people to ensure that the activities and thought processes of their everyday lives were so deeply seated that there would be no possibility of any change in society. Yet the notion of '**not doing anything**' interrupts ordinary thought, by introducing a momentary state of chaos: from this comes greater fluidity of thought and action.

Shift the way you put on your shoes.

Even though you find your feet, do not get upset as you walk in your shoes in this new way.

To break up the cycle of routine, in the sense of '**doing nothing**', Don Juan gave Castaneda some exercises so that he could develop some awareness of those very routines. Some of those exercises were necessarily backward looking, as if looking in a mirror. One of them was to wear clothes back to front. All such techniques were aimed at making Castaneda aware of everything that was happening to him at every single moment. As he broke with those old routines, he found his body open to new sensations.

the way forward

In order to go forward in an orderly way it is necessary to have one's hands free. If carrying something, the best way is to lift it onto the shoulders. The fingers have to be hooked, or else be in an unusual position. The eyes, focused on no particular point, have to look toward the route that leads from the feet to somewhere above the horizon. This extended view can be something of a relief: it enables a person to capture details that are generally too fleeting for our regular way of seeing to grasp. This serves to halt internal dialogue, reasoning with oneself, and so shifts one's focus on the world at large.

The body knows well just what it is capable of.

In this way one can safely run through the night.

The workings of power have a special way of going forward, through shadows and darkness.

Castaneda learned the games of the Toltec tradition, in which there are no fixed rules, but which are played in the way that is most practicable at the time.

Given that the style of the players cannot be forecast, everyone has to be very alert and attentive.

One particular game entailed giving false signals to the opponent. It was a game rather like archery.

I am about to learn a few things,

Use all your resources against that force. Otherwise you will be drowned in repetition and boredom.

For the shamans of ancient Mexico, those who 'did nothing' were always closely connected with their magical powers. For Don Juan, the stagnation that stems from the framework of doing — action — must be characteristic of the majority of people. They confront all situations following a circular movement of energy. Therefore everything is repeated. There is nothing new, and there is no expansion.

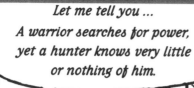

Let me tell you ...
A warrior searches for power,
yet a hunter knows very little
or nothing of him.

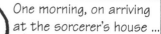

One morning, on arriving
at the sorcerer's house ...

Speak to me of power,
Don Juan.

Personal power determines
the way in which one does things.
A person is the sum of personal
power.

The decision to be a warrior or a hunter stems from the world of the powers that guide humankind. Don Juan was both warrior and hunter ...

Then Castaneda returned once more to the United States. After several months of not seeing the shaman, he started to prepare for yet another visit to Don Juan in Sonora.

Don Juan saw Castaneda as having made some advances along the way of learning, but still the developments of all those years would have to be consolidated.

It was important that Castaneda should commit himself to his own personal power. According to the sorcerer, all that we might be and might do can rest only in that power. If one does not have power for oneself, whatever revelations may occur would then be worthless.

The shifts and changes that happen within your life

the art of participating in dreams

Don Juan instructed Castaneda in the art of conjuring up the stuff of dreams, one of the core issues of Toltec sorcery.

By means of this skill, a person can arrive at a special level of attention, the so-called '**second concentration**'. The practice of conjuring is one of the ways of amplifying perception. To conjure up the stuff of dreams is not simply to be able to remember the dreams that all of us have and many of us share — even though those dreams are gateways to other environments. Participating in dreams means to learn how to dream on purpose, at will, and in a systematic way.

It begins by dreaming with one's own hand and fingers. Next, all of the arm is involved. This continues progressively to take over a person's body completely, so that oneself can be observed as another person, as in a dream. The ability to keep consciousness fixed on the elements of a dream is called *concentration on dreaming*. Once dreams can be controlled, participation in them can be acquired.

For instance, you can dream that you leave your body and walk out into the street ... then you can change yourself into something beyond apprehension.

It *is* possible to live through much in dreams.

Castaneda realised that dreaming does not happen on the timescale of ordinary clocks and watches. As opposed to ordinary dreams, which are simply runaway imagination, there are others that are governors of energy — those allow us to see how that energy flows from the universe ...

For the shaman, one of the advantages to be gained in progressing with the skill of dreaming is that internal dialogue, reasoning with oneself, is slowed down, even suspended.

less chance of perceiving that there are many other worlds, each of them possible.

Internal dialogue is the reaffirmation that people continually make of their description of the world. By the same token, they maintain a certain level of efficiency, keeping themselves in order.

There is a certain description of the world, not altogether arbitrary, hammered out by priests and leaders alike. Repeated often enough, by means of internal dialogue, that message means that there is

The key to sorcery is to shift the idea one has of the world and so to halt interior dialogue.

For the sorcerers, many ordinary people may well continue to converse with themselves, internally, in isolation. The same things will be repeated, facts and events that may have been said and done before, which people may have some sense of or no longer feel at all.

When internal dialogue is interrupted, there opens automatically a new gateway.

Shall I tell them what happened to me?

... but you don't believe

that to be aware of doubts and fears is the mark of a sensitive man.

At this stage, Castaneda could not withdraw, because it was too late. Nor could he go into action, because it was too soon. He would have to become a witness to the actions of power, to listen to Don Juan's tales of power.

Castaneda refuted his own earlier opinions in his fourth book, **Tales of Power** (1974).

We all confuse ourselves on purpose ...

Before revealing the essential secret of the sorcerers, they made Castaneda solve a kind of riddle, to show that he had amassed enough power to receive the knowledge.

He had to meet with Don Genaro without knowing when or where to find him.

there he is!

Castaneda consolidated his power to see.

One night, while talking with the sorcerer, he heard a kind of buzzing, which took him by surprise.

For you, the insect represents knowledge.

You have learned for yourself that we are luminous beings. We are a sensation. What we call the body is a thread of luminous fibres where awareness shines.

Another day he saw Don Genaro demonstrating his skills at the foot of a tree. The necessary ability stretched him to his limits. His will might have failed, but not his reason.

Don Juan pointed out that a seer is is somebody who observes human beings as very fine filaments of light, which spiral from the head to the navel. He saw a human being potentially as a luminous seed or globe. The arms and legs are like shining bristles that spring out on all sides.

Every person is in contact with his or her surroundings by means of a vast number of long threads that lead from the centre of the abdomen. These threads connect with one another and give a person equilibrium.

Being able to see in this way, a person is a luminous seed, with that power, whether rich or poor, a beggar or a king.

What makes a person into a luminous seed?

For the shaman, to see is the guiding principle of shamanism.

And perceiving – something more unusual – is interpreting the flow of energy without the influence of the mind. Freed from the mind, the interpretation of sensory data becomes something not concerned with facts. So, the body, in its entirety, contributes to this new perception like a cluster of energy fields.

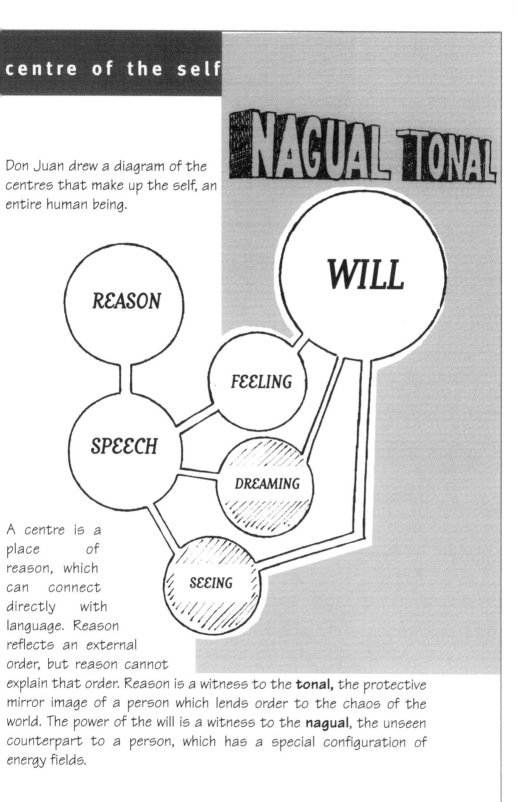

Don Juan drew a diagram of the centres that make up the self, an entire human being.

A centre is a place of reason, which can connect directly with language. Reason reflects an external order, but reason cannot explain that order. Reason is a witness to the **tonal,** the protective mirror image of a person which lends order to the chaos of the world. The power of the will is a witness to the **nagual**, the unseen counterpart to a person, which has a special configuration of energy fields.

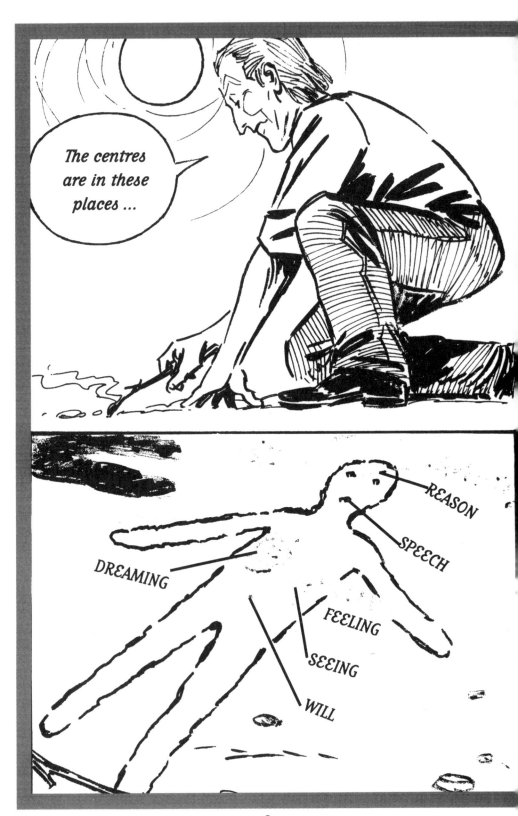

the two rings

The sorcerer explained that tangible objects are the means to guide us more easily through our time on earth.

Luminous beings are born with two rings of power. One is reason, which together with language maintains the world as it is. The other is will, the ring the sorcerers use and that humankind in general does not. Will is also a means of seeing and describing the world, which has rules and regulations of its own.

a challenge

Don Juan presented Castaneda with a challenge.

He would have to make himself aware of what it had been that upheld his own description of the world, of everyday life — that definition which gave him a determined image and form ...
Did it uphold reason?
or will ?

*Accepting this challenge would lead to the accumulation of personal power,
and so to the achievement of oneself, in one's own entirety.*

an encounter with power

One day Castaneda was browsing among the secondhand bookstalls of Mexico City.

Suddenly he ran into Don Juan. What surprised Castaneda most of all was

that Don Juan was impeccably dressed in a suit! He felt he had come to the end of a road, that anything was possible.

You took on life as a challenge, you connected with personal power ... and so you have met me without our having made an appointment.

The main difference between a warrior and an ordinary human being is that the first takes on everything as a challenge, and the second sees life either as a curse or a blessing.

Whether warriors or not, people do have a little bit of luck that comes their way from time to time. An ordinary human being is in general too much occupied, worried or too lazy to take account or advantage of that.

The sorcerers said that the universe accessible to perception is like an onion bulb, something that has very many concentric layers. Our everyday world is just one of those layers.

A warrior is floating,

he adapts to changes ...

And he has to believe ...

How is that?

It means taking account of everything. To have to believe that the world is mysterious and unfathomable — that is the most essential undertaking of a warrior.

The *tonal* is the regulator of the world. Everything we may know or do is the work of the *tonal*. Its function is to impose order on chaos. It works like a control, as a guardian who may become intolerant. There is a personal tonal and a collective one also, the *tonal* of all time.

You can imagine the TONAL as living on an island, like this table, with all of the things spread out upon it.

the nagual

It is the part of ourselves that we never deal with. It cannot be described ... but it can be witnessed.

It lies beyond, where power is to be found. At birth we are all nagual. Then we feel we are missing something. In time we develop into integrated tonal, and still we feel incomplete. We can see that there is another side, but the tonal is in control and will not let us perceive it.

However, there are moments when the control of the tonal is loosened: that is when the entirety of a human being may make itself apparent.

Then you can imagine the NAGUAL as everything that is not spread out upon this table.

Don Juan taught Castaneda how to recognise the tonal in other people and so see what they are really like.

When a man passed by, wearing a suit and perspiring ...

*There is no need to treat the body
in such an appalling way.
But we all learn how to weaken ourselves.
I call that giving way to vice.*

The sorcerer did all he could to restrict Castaneda's *tonal*, so as to give way to the marvellous insights of the *nagual*. Don Juan and Don Genaro spoke to Castaneda at every opportunity about another technique for improving perception, given the name of '*partir*', meaning 'leaving', 'departure', 'taking off'.

Don Juan, as Castaneda's **MASTER,** helped him by explaining everything connected with the **TONAL.** Don Genaro was Castaneda's **BENEFACTOR,** that is to say, the one who would demonstrate the power of the **NAGUAL** and the way to reach it.

Don Genaro also had two other apprentices, Pablito and Nestor. For them, it was Don Juan who was the benefactor.

The human body, seen as energy, is composed of two complementary forces. They are the right hand body and the left hand body, which reflect the dual structure of the universe.

Now I don't have so many questions to ask.

With all that Castaneda was living through and putting into practice, he managed to spread his wings, in terms of his own perception. Leaving behind ordinary understanding, he rose to inconceivable levels. And he could see even further ...

He returned to Los Angeles yet again and put his notes in order once more. He was excited to the point that certain changes were taking place within himself.

For several months he had not allowed himself to be disturbed. He had made no concessions to himself in facing up to the tasks ahead. Soon he felt that it was time to visit the sorcerers again. As never before, he was anchored in present time.

Castaneda was now ready to receive the knowledge. We see ourselves reflected in a globe — such is our view of the world. Whenever the benefactor breaks the surface of the globe from the outside, the master remodels that view of the world and prepares the way for the luminous being, The break in the surface, where the benefactor has torn it apart, allows the luminous being to be seen in its entirety. The master gathers together the fragments on the right hand side of the opening — the side where reason and the tonal reside. So the left hand side is left free — where the power of the will resides, so that the benefactor can open the globe completely.

The right hand body is the dominant one. Its preference is noise.

The left hand body is more effective in sorcery. It prefers silence.

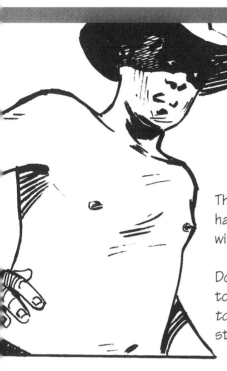

Human beings and other luminous entities are the ones who perceive. That is the secret of the luminous beings.
It is wrong to believe that everythinghappens only at the centreof the power of reason.

Therefore the sorcerers' explanations had to be concerned with spreading the wings of the power of reason ...

Don Juan and Don Genaro worked toward Castaneda's passing from the *tonal* to the *nagual* in several linked stages.

In an alternating mode, from one stage to another, Castaneda had the experience of his consciousness being fragmented. So he began to have visions.

Endowed with the wings of perception, it is possible to fly to other worlds than our own, to other planets, to the realms of the *tonal* and the *nagual*.

You yourself, along with Pablito, will go together and alone into the unknown.

The best way to bid farewell is with a memory of joyfulness.

Castaneda and Pablito had to pass into the *tonal* and then the *nagual* with the strength of their own personal power. Nestor was their witness.

Don Juan and Don Genaro set them on their way. Castaneda sensed a moment of insecurity and of intense loneliness, but he was able to take charge of himself.

That was the last time he saw Don Juan and Don Genaro, and so his apprenticeship to them came to an end.

Before taking his leap forward, Castaneda felt Pablito supporting him by the arm.

After that he was alone.

the leap forward

This was the decisive moment. The question — as to whether or not Castaneda should leap into an abyss — could be answered only by somebody speaking from a particular standpoint: only by somebody with the same world view held by the same person who might have formulated that same question.

For example — had he ever flown before, like a crow, on those occasions when he had been smoking those 'sacred weeds'?

For the shaman, the leap and the taking off (and the marvels of other worlds) are distinct from the emptiness of the abyss and the flight of the crow. Their difference cannot be the same as any distinction, that may be made between them, in the systems of thought common in the western world. But they are not for that reason any the less real. For the shaman however, those differences and distinctions are irrelevant and absurd.

Again, according to the shamans, Castaneda could transform himself into a being of pure perception, only after having taken the *leap*. So, many times more than once, he was swinging between the *tonal* and the *nagual*.

Castaneda could follow a thread through his experiences of sorcery, but he felt that his own reasoning would make him refuse to take the leap. However, another part of himself held on to the conviction that he should undertake that next move.

He had to go forward in the midst of contradictions. His task consisted of taking stock of whatever he had learned from the sorcerers. He went back to Mexico to disentangle himself from his confusion.

He wanted to see Pablito and Nestor.

What happened next had a deep effect upon his reasoning.

He discovered that Pablito and Nestor were part of a larger group of men and women who were apprentices of Don Juan and Don Genaro.

The sorcerers have been keeping me apart from the rest of them.

They told Castaneda that he was to be their guide, the nagual of the whole group. They were all to take the name of 'the flight of the new nagual'. The women took violent exception to Castaneda, which for him was almost cathartic. From then on his understanding was to be radically changed.

Florinda is very powerful.

According to Don Juan, women have more talent than men and are more sensitive. The way of knowledge lies open to women.

Moreover, they waste their energies less and do not tire as easily as men do.

Don Juan had left Castaneda in the hands of a Toltec woman named Florinda, who would carry on as his teacher.

We may not be about to go leaping into the abyss, but we have tasks that are more difficult.

Castaneda was told that another advantage that women have is their receptivity. As receivers, they can also receive knowledge, a characteristic which is also related to the fact that women are bearers of children.

Women, as opposed to men, do not have to be pressed into setting out upon the way of the warrior ... Women may enter freely into everything. Paradoxically, this is supposed to be their great weakness!

Furthermore, women are supposed to be more equipped than men, when faced with the gulf between different worlds or perceptions. This sensibility and sensitivity is due to women's menstrual cycle.

Women, they say, have to be contained, whilst men must be given guidance.

Human patterns are luminous entities, the source and origin of all people. As well as human beings, plants and animals each have their own patterns also.

The human pattern is the same for all of us, but it manifests itself and takes effect in different ways, according to individual development.

Castaneda saw the image of our pattern as having a human shape. Others might see it as a beam of light.

When we gather enough power, we can perceive the pattern, which some might see as a deity.

A warrior has to free himself from form, if he truly wishes to develop. Human beings are addicted to the idea that theirs is the only interpretative system that exists. Having left that behind, there is no energy left for old habits. Without those, it is possible to pass over to the other side, to another way of seeing.

Commonly held ideas about love were no longer shared by Castaneda, not in romantic terms, nor in any weak and sentimental way. He stated that it had cost him much to learn that, because he had previously been romantically inclined and he had shared the general notion of always searching for love, instead of realising that all that people want, in fact, is to satisfy their sexual needs.

It is possible to love with no hope of response, remaining unconcerned. That comes from not asking for anything.

We believe we can love too much, because we expect too much and so we feel grief ... but in truth that need not be so — to think so is an egoist's pose.

Do I please you? Do you love me?

Castaneda had learned from Don Juan to refuse the egoist's pose of going about the world searching for love, like a slave to other people's opinions. He had learned to value himself for himself.

Everything stems from that, from a state of solitude.

Groups of apprentices lead very austere lives.Sex wastes energies that are needed for other tasks.

For Castaneda, children born of casual and careless sexual activity do not grow up to have much energy within themselves.He saw that modern civilisation causes most people's sexual activity to be categorised in this way. People are mostly discontent, suffering from anxiety, constantly searching for excitements of which they feel deprived.This places them in the difficult position of needing to conserve their energies by abstaining from sex. But that position is on a par with the situation in which certain people find themselves, having been more favourably born out of passionate circumstances.

The sexual act is of tremendous importance.
It consumes a great deal of energy and is designed principally for procreation.
It cannot be squandered in a banal fashion.
There is nothing wrong with human sensuality,
but there is something wrong in the ignorance that leads people
to overlook their own magical nature.

From the point of view
of the material world
lifestyles and relationships among a group of apprentices go unobserved.
Speaking for myself, it took me a long time to understand that.

Nothing in life is irrevocable.
It is always possible to give back those
things that do not
belong to us and to recover
those things that do.

I gave back my cutting edge
to my mother and father
and so I recovered my own.

When human beings reproduce themselves, they lose their special 'cutting edge'. This is a power that children inherit from their parents, by the simple fact of being born.

The empty space left behind, within a parent, by the loss of the cutting edge is one that must be filled or recovered.

Nevertheless, there are other circumstances which can compensate for this loss. A parent can discover repose. Also, those who have brought children into the world can often know well how to care for others.

Castaneda was sure that all true Toltecs are born of a group that has kept alive a tradition going back thousands of years.

The term *Toltec* does not refer here to the Toltec nation in an anthropological sense. It refers to a person endowed with knowledge. The word infers the transmission of mysteries.

> A Toltec is a person who knows the mysteries of ambush and of dreaming. The seers are those who can perceive people as globes of light.

Don Juan was the leader of the party of the 'old' *nagual*, a group of only fifteen people. He was also the guide for a group of nine apprentice seers. So, their leader was Castaneda himself.

To leave the living world.
To leave with all that one has become,
but with nothing more than who one is.

The issue is: to take nothing nor
to leave anything.

• We are those who perceive. To perceive was ever our original intention.

• We are our own beginning. The amount of a person's energy is, in principle, decided by the passion felt by the parents at the moment of orgasm, of conception.

• Perception has to be conceived in its entirety. That is to say, with physical capacities, faculties and energy — all gathered together as one.

Over the years, Don Juan had given Castaneda various definitions of sorcery. Those definitions change at the pace of increasing knowledge. Towards the end of his apprenticeship, Castaneda was shown how sorcery is a specialised use of energy.

Therefore it is possible to learn how to stock up on energy, and so to control energy fields that could not previously have been accessible.

the four steps

There are four steps along the path of knowledge.

1. Ordinary people turn themselves into apprentices.

2. They change their minds about themselves and the world. They become able to discipline themselves to the maximum. Then they turn themselves into warriors.

3. They acquire the skill, and then refine it, to choose the opportune moment to pass on and so become people of knowledge.

4. They learn to see and are transformed into seers.

This is a Toltec figure.

The overall view of the ancient shamans (embracing life, the universe and consciousness) hangs upon the existence of an indescribable power. Metaphorically, it is called the **Eagle**. It is given this name because the seer perceives it as a vast dark shadow extending to infinity, crossed by a flash of lightning. It is also known as the dark sea of consciousness.

This force lends energy to all living things, from the tiniest virus to the status of a human being. It gives consciousness to the newborn. This will enhance the experience of life itself. Living things die because they have to give back their consciousness, full grown over time, to the power that gave it to them while they were living.

The Eagle has no pity. Everything that is alive is represented within it. It embraces all the beauty and bestiality of which human beings are capable.

Compared to the little substance that a human being has, the Eagle has enormous mass ...

The Eagle attracts every living force that is about to disappear. The Eagle is like a giant magnet that draws together every single beam of light.

It is necessary to approach the Eagle as closely as possible and to find a way to evade it so that it does not swallow us up.
The way of a warrior's knowledge is lengthy and requires total dedication.

... because an impeccable being can change one's destiny, and so one can leave on tiptoe along the Eagle's left hand side ...

There are shamans who manage the feat of saving their own lives, by passing on, to the Eagle, the power of their extended knowledge — gained through their own life experiences. Those shamans transcend death by retaining their own vital strength. Yet they disappear from the face of the earth, embarking upon a consummate journey of perception.

According to the Toltecs, whatever relates to the Eagle has to be returned to it.

The **Eagle** is the governor of humankind, because it feeds on the vital energy that frees ourselves. There is an offering that can be made to the **Eagle**. It is known as personal recapitulation or appraisal. This can help to construct a platform for reaching a level of silent understanding.

To appraise oneself in this way is to recapitulate and recapture moments and events, reliving them. It necessitates recovering all previous experiences. First, a list has to be drawn up of all the people one has known throughout one's life. This must include all those who have pressed us to put the ego to the fore.

I put aside all those who have conspired to make us participate in the game of '... love me ... love me not ...'.

The recapitulation has to be all embracing, and it must be carried out with unwavering willpower. It begins with the present and leads back to earliest childhood.

Images are conjured up and they must remain fixed in the mind. But, with a turn of the head from right to left, each of those images has to be blown away, obliterated from our view ... the breath that blows them away is magical.

One has been at the mercy of forces which, although they may have seemed reasonable, were in the end absurd.

So, as the sorcerers say, the feelings recovered from those past times time are to be taken in, with our breathing. But when we breathe out, we rid ourselves of those undesirable states of mind that were contained within such moments.

By recounting such moments to ourselves, extraordinary strength can be acquired. That is because random energy can be redistributed through our centres.

This allows free-flowing power to be collected together, when we have given over to the Eagle all that we have held close to us.

Such fluidity is achieved because appraisal of ourselves and reliving our life experiences have caused our point of leverage to shift, to be adjusted.

At the end of this recapitulation, the games come to an end, as do all the tricks and deceptions.

Following upon self appraisal, and so stripped of one's ego, the task of the Toltec remains free to be accomplished. This demands absolutely everything of a person.

Castaneda had to learn to distance himself from solemnity and to become more lighthearted ...

In carrying out tasks of this kind, many things that are connected with practical situations in everyday life can be discovered and tackled.

There are always opportunities of seeing how to transmit knowledge.

With a little subtlety, the spoken word is always helpful ... ... everyone who faithfully carries out the task can make good use of speaking.

All living things are capable of learning. Everyone has the chance of living like a warrior. The only requirement is to remain implacable in the desire to be free.

Florinda, the Toltec elder, was the one in charge of handing out tasks to the group of apprentices.

Everyone had tasks to fulfil, on different occasions. Castaneda carried out his tasks together with an apprentice named Elena, nicknamed La Gorda — the Fat One.

...he of Florinda's ways of teaching was to put the apprentices into tricky situations.

That is the best way. That is how we find that we are reduced to nothing.

We discover we are nothing ... or we carry on following the fashion of self esteem, of taking pride in ourselves. In that case, we are always paying attention to whatever may happen to us or upset us. We become detectives, looking for signs of whether people care for us or not.
Concerned only with the ego, We become something different from whatever may lend us strength.

The best thing to do is to begin thinking that nobody cares for us.

From that time — when he had already gained considerable recognition and fame — Castaneda spent some years fulfilling various tasks, in very demanding and adverse conditions. Then he changed his name and his way of recording things. He began to call himself Joe Cordoba or Joe Cortes.

One of the tasks he had to perform was as a roadside barbecue jerk. Elena went with him as his assistant, and he presented her as his wife.

José Luis Córdoba, at your service.

They worked like that for a year. Meanwhile, another girl was taken on, named Terry.

Castaneda is out there, in that automobile.

Why don't you talk to him?

I don't have the nerve ... I'm so ugly.

But you're lovely ... go on ...

During those years, Castaneda went through times of great deprivation. He was constantly badly treated and abused. But that was the stage, on his way forward, where he could 'touch down to earth' and 'be as nothing'. It was also a stage linked to the process of further initiation, which had begun with Don Juan. It was a process of losing personal importance. More than once he was on the point of speaking out, of saying who he was, but he went forward according to the decisions that Florinda had imposed upon him.

The tasks that Castaneda accomplished with Elena were lessons in surviving in the face of adversity. Those tasks were closely related to the experiences of taking risks, of shrewd judgment, of astuteness. Such circumstances can be very hard to bear, but they can also be very edifying.

Some time later Florinda urged Castaneda's group to go into business on a rather grand scale, designing and laying out gardens.

One day, when they were visiting a friend, some journalists arrived, looking for Castaneda.

So as to pass unnoticed, the apprentices took up their work in the garden. Their friend, keeping up appearances, shouted at them and berated them, in front of the journalists, none of whom intervened to defend them.

For three years, Castaneda and Elena continued with those tasks, tests and trials, so as to benefit from physical experiences, to develop healthy bodies. That made them sufficiently aware, to be able to say that ...

... in truth they were as nothing.
Not only the body suffers.
The mind also becomes used
to constant pressure.
But the warrior has no need
to be stimulated by simple things.

until when?

So, to find oneself in this position is to become self sufficient.

For a time, the group found work as domestics. They were fired without being paid, and reported to the police.

Then for one year, without the support of the group, Castaneda and Elena found themselves alone. Often they went without food.

One object of being tried and tested is to learn how to avoid the emotional impact of being despised, discriminated against. The important thing is not to react, not to take offence, so as not to lose one's grip.

One does not seek to defend oneself against
a tiger about to attack. One steps aside and
allows the tiger to pass.

In **The Second Ring of Power** (1977), Castaneda narrates his experiences on returning to Mexico.

The following books appeared later:

* **The Eagle's Gift** (1981);
* **The Fire from Within** (1984);
* **The Power of Silence** (1987);
* **The Art of Dreaming** (1993);

also:

* **Interior Silence** (1998) a publication that is not widely known, circulated amongst Castaneda's followers;

and finally:

* **Magical Passes** (1998)

> *I am just a bridge to the world. All the knowledge in my books belongs to the Toltec nation.*

Writing is above all a shamanic challenge. Castaneda sought to transmit another vision of reality, and furthermore to restore dignity to a culture extinguished by the Spanish conquest of ancient Mexico. Writing is not simply work. It is a task, a test and a trial which consists of capturing the kind of page — like a rubric or a message — that is received in dreams. The success of each particular page depends on the faithfulness with which the model of the dream is copied down.

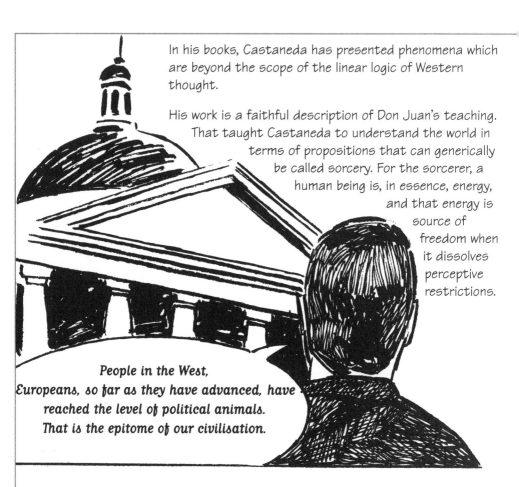

In his books, Castaneda has presented phenomena which are beyond the scope of the linear logic of Western thought.

His work is a faithful description of Don Juan's teaching. That taught Castaneda to understand the world in terms of propositions that can generically be called sorcery. For the sorcerer, a human being is, in essence, energy, and that energy is source of freedom when it dissolves perceptive restrictions.

People in the West, Europeans, so far as they have advanced, have reached the level of political animals. That is the epitome of our civilisation.

In June 1973, Don Juan passed over to another world of perception, together with Don Genaro. But they remain present in the writings of Carlos Castaneda.

The sorcerer's teachings are based on the fact that humankind has two kinds of consciousness: one on the right and one on the left, each path having its own method of instruction. Castaneda received the knowledge of the right hand path, in a state of regular, ordinary, normal consciousness.

The teachings of the left hand path are received each time one enters into a unique state of clear perception, which is called advanced consciousness.

For years the shaman had made Castaneda enter ino such states. He did this with a blow of the hand on the upper part of the back, between the shoulderblades.

> Now you'll see!

One's conduct, in a state of advanced consciousness, is as natural as in everyday life.

The advantage of being in such a state is that one can focus the mind, with great force and clarity, on anything whatsoever. The mundane context of this is reduced to the minimum. That is because total concentration is occupied with the details of that particular moment's activity.

The disadvantage of advanced consciousness lies in the difficulty of holding whatever happens within regular memory. Events become part of everyday memory only by means of considerable effort.

Without sadness and longing for times past, one is incomplete, because from those feelingscome feelings of sobriety, gentleness.

In these conditions, Castaneda was also interacting with other seers, members of Don Juan's group.

Castaneda had feelings of great joy and of freedom. But he also had feelings of sadness and loneliness, nostalgia.

readers of the infinite

According to Don Juan, this is a phenomenological description, referring to a certain state of perception known to the shamans. This condition is in accord with the aims of those people who read books of special interest. Such texts may take the form of a book, a file on a computer screen, a guidebook, works of literature, technical studies, etc.

Words appear clearly as soon as they are read. They form concepts that manifest themselves and at once disappear.

The art of the shaman is to reunite and to preserve those concepts, before they are forgotten, so as to be replaced with new words and concepts in an endless flow of graphic consciousness.

The ancient shamans discovered that once having advanced to the level of interior silence, consciousness can easily leap into direct perception of energy, as reflected at a point on the horizon. The horizon they referred to could be the sky, the line of a mountain range, even the roof of a house. They could see the reflected energy as a point of a crimson colour, as if it were a film across the eye, a scale or a cataract. This transformed the shamans into spectators, observers, readers of the infinite.

According to Don Juan, Castaneda was a reader of the infinite, by virtue of the passion with which he could read.

silent knowledge

This is the teaching to be received in a state of advanced consciousness. In such a state, the sorcerer can ontain knowledge of all that is relevant to humankind directly, from his own intentions, in an instantaneous fashion, without any intervention of the spoken language.

The prelude to silent knowledge is interior silence. It is a state free of thought and verbalisation, even in silence, free of internal dialogue. In such a state, there is no more need for the everyday cognitive system. Indescribable levels can be reached, which are different from the worlds that can be entered by participating in dreams.

For the way to arrive at interior silence, there are no guidebooks, no manuals, no procedures to follow. All that is needed is to be quiet, even for a few seconnds, and to persevere. To manage this, to get there, just the intention is necessary, to want it, navigating the waters of the unknown.

This specific knowledge, difficult to understand, is passed from generation to generation of sorcerers ...

Those with the power of the nagual, those that are called the guides, are people endowed with great energy and extraordinary qualities. Their luminous globe is composed of four segments. They are intermediaries for the intentions. In most people, they awaken the consciousness of their own connections with their intentions.

It can take a whole lifetime to remember everything that is perceived and understood within silent knowledge, to translate it in terms of reasoning.

Cosmic forces and silent knowledge can open up to us a world of demons.

Rationality may bring us tranquillity. But that tranquillity of everyday life cannot be sustained ...

We have to return to silent knowledge, but yet with less fear.

... now we return with a trophy: understanding.

This is the place in the human body responsible for the taking of decisions. It is the 'V' point, located at the top of the breastbone, at the base of the throat and neck. It is also known as the liquid centre.

The shamans isolated and identified the incapacity of humankind, across the centuries, to make decisions for themselves. It is for this reason that vast organisations were created to assume that responsibility, for making decisions.

People left social institutions to make choices on their behalf and then to act on those decisions, taken in the name of the people. But that centre of energy, along with the five other most important centres that the human body possesses, could be put to use, to perceive energy directly. Those magical passes and movements are at present to be studied in Castaneda's own organisation, which is known as Tensegrity.

Those movements are reinforced constantly. So, the energy dispersed by everyday waste can be renewed. All doubt about taking decisions can be resolved.

The other centres of energy are located at these sites:

- the liver and the duodenum;
- the pancreas and the spleen;
- the kidneys and the endocrine system;
- the womb;
- the crown of the head.

Without an adversary, we are nothing.
To be an adversary is part of the human condition.
Life is war. Life is struggle.
Peace is something unusual.

Referring to pacifism, Castaneda called it a monstrosity. This was because he considered humankind to be creatures of competition and struggle. Apparently, for Castaneda the term 'pacifism' had connotations of lack of energy and lack of objectives. He saw it as a complacent attitude.

However, Castaneda did not regard Gandhi (1869-1948) as a pacifist. Rather, he saw Gandhi as one of the most amazing fighters that had ever existed.

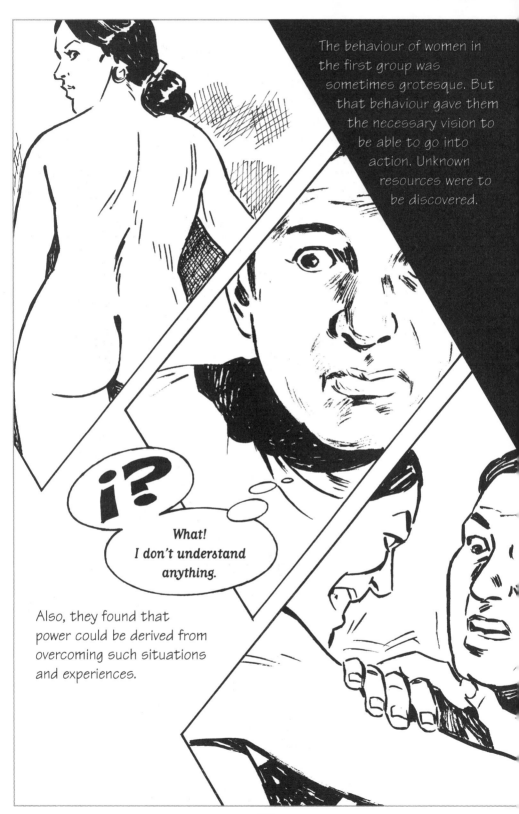

The behaviour of women in the first group was sometimes grotesque. But that behaviour gave them the necessary vision to be able to go into action. Unknown resources were to be discovered.

What! I don't understand anything.

Also, they found that power could be derived from overcoming such situations and experiences.

It is not easy to dream ...
It improves with practice.

There were not always fights and shouting matches among the group. Castaneda, with his notebook always handy, revised some of his teachings and reinforced other lessons.

Also, when practising dreaming together with the women, Castaneda expanded his perception of the second, advanced order.

Pragmatism is a strength demonstrated to Castaneda by Don Juan. The shamans had been searching for the enhancement of the consciousness of being on an ever grander scale. This meant being able to perceive with all the capacities that, as a luminous being, a person could muster – not just with some of those skills.

Therefore the sorcerer rejected the idea of spirituality. In reality, putting their pretensions aside, Western people are not pragmatists: nor are they objective, nor are they spiritual.

Castaneda understood that he could insist on the word spiritual as an opposition to the greed of the everyday commercial world, by naming that greed as spirituality.

Faced with the emptiness of the idea of spirituality – which seems attractive because it is based on literary and poetical concepts – the shamans have taken up their positions.

We are all going to enter into infinity.
Why not do so now? – while we are alive and strong.
We have to face the infinite in a practical way, without ideals and without deities.

without words

There are some things that cannot be explained. Because the answers to certain questions are to be found in practice and not in intellectual theorising, we have to act. To explain can mean the dissipation of energy in sterile efforts.

Moreover, in order to speak, one must use the syntax of the language. The force of that syntax and its usage limits the possibilities of expression. It refers only to the perception of the world in which we are living.

Leaving the tree as it is, so that it may become pure energy, is a pragmatic piece of handiwork.

Florinda, the sorcerer looking after Don Juan's group, was directing and teaching a group of her own. Also, over twelve years, she was with Castaneda's group, which she had organised originally. She passed to a higher state in 1985.

Castaneda's group had included:

- Florinda Donner-Grau, named after the Toltec sorceress and also known as Gina (herself a sorceress of great standing)
- Taisha Abelar (a teacher of dreaming)
- Carol Tiggs (a woman of the nagual)

Carol Tiggs was the feminine counterpart of Castaneda, a woman of parallel energy. Those three people had known Don Juan personally, but they had carried different male names:

- Melchor Yaoquizque
- John Michel Abelar
- Mariano Aureliano

They were known as the 'old nagual', because of their long standing rather than their age, whilst Castaneda was known as the 'new nagual'.

Castaneda recounted at length his experiences with Don Juan's group, and with the first apprentices, as agreed with the shaman. So, it was some time before Castaneda took on the second group.

> Nobody wants to be wholly part of it.

The number of people in the group had to be a multiple of four. That was the standard required for a group to function. Eight was the most effective number, because that had the effect of creating a small mass of people and breaking with individualism.

To deal with a group of nine people would be an arduous undertaking and would call for a special kind of energy.

The second group was much more compact. They had all been apprentices of Don Juan. Another common characteristic was that all of them had been university students, as well as being followers of the shaman. Both directions came together along the same path. They were historians, anthropologists, bibliographers ...

Florinda Donner-Grau (who had received not only her name but other powerful attributes from the Toltec sorceress) was, like Castaneda, an anthropologist.

Intellectual preparation was a precondition that Don Juan had laid down, and that became part of the way of the warrior. So, Castaneda held on to his inclination toward an academic career.

He recognised the attraction that academic circles held for him, although he rejected the commonplaces and routine structures of that lifestyle.

> *The intellect is the only faculty that can safeguard against fear and the inevitable tidal wave of the unknown.*

> *The intellect is the only faculty that can be a consolation to the sorcerer. Consolation does not come from the sorcerer's fire nor from other such sentiments — it is the intellect that saves the sorcerer.*

The word attention became Castaneda's term for a special kind of concentration. It is a capacity which he felt to be characteristic of human beings. It comes as a result, finally, of having cultivated a particular physical activity – perception. There are alternatives, which can be chosen according to one's social surroundings, but they have their limitations. Chances of success derive from whatever can be achieved by luminous beings.

There are three levels of knowledge, of attention. Each one has its own independent domain, complete in itself.

> Attention is the act of engaging and channelling perception.

This becomes evident in childhood. A a kind of attention, it is distinct from the concentration that affects adults and those who have mastered knowledge. By means of this first attention, the world is perceived as having a determinate form. Other perceptual possibilities are rejected. It allows the human body to be appreciated, along with the objects that make up everyday life, just as we see them.

A table is a table, whether it's here or anywhere!

This attention requires a determination to interpret perception in a specific way, according to a consensus among those who share that determination.

New seers have several names for the accepted emanations that comprise perception: the right hand path, regular consciousness, the tonal, this world, that which is known, the first concentration.

Ordinary people have other names for perception: reality, rationality, common sense.

The effects of 'doing nothing' are operations that can hamper the regular focus of the first concentration.

Also, the strength of intention, as a current of energy, can eventually be slowed down or reorientated.

the second kind of attention

The effects of 'doing nothing', and the conduct of intention, are ways to reach the level of the second attention, which is that of advanced consciousness, also known as consciousness of the left hand path, the nagual, the other world or the unknown. This attention is governed by strict parameters. To reach it implies, beyond the desire to enter into other worlds, some adequate distribution of energy. Castaneda explained his own leap into the abyss and the departure of the sorcerers to another world as passages to this other consciousness and attention.

People do have an effective ability to enter into those worlds, which are just as real, unique and absorbing as our own everyday lives.

Other very important ways to pass into other realms are the practices handed down by the ancient sorcerers, through the art of dreaming.

Dreaming is the gateway to the infinite.

the third kind of attention

To secure the total freedom that this attention can bring is a goal that the warrior actively pursues. It requires the greatest mastery and impeccability. There are special instances of this, experienced only by the seers. In these instances they have an inner fire. That inner fire consumes them. In full consciousness, they merge with the great emanations of the Eagle, and spread throughout eternity.

Crossing over into freedom does not signify eternal life as eternity is generally understood.

It is conserving consciousness whilst crossing over and entering into the third attention. The body is inflamed with knowledge.

It is entering into an evolutionary process, using the only means that we have at our disposal: consciousness.

intention

This strength is present everywhere and enables us to perceive. To the extent that it exists in the cosmos, it is joined to its source by a vital link. The sorcerers have shown great interest in understanding that link and utilising it, in cleansing it of the adverse effects of everyday concerns.

The shamans define themselves for themselves, as navigators of the waters of the unknown. There can be no procedures or steps to follow, other than a single abstract act: tightening the knot with the force that is known as intention.

We perceive as a result of the pressure and intrusion of the intention (or spirit).

The sorcerers consider this impersonal strength to be the basis of the universe. It is that which determines the sorcerer's activity and output, whatever those practices may be.

Intention is, also, a prowess that can be acquired.

Given the knowledge that there are emanations on a large scale, as well as emanations within the luminous seed, and that both are aligned in the act of perceiving, the new seers developed techniques to maintain that alignment.

The energy that surges up from this conjunction is known as the will. It is a detonator. It is impersonal. It cannot be defused. It makes us carry ourselves according to that explosion which we have ourselves set off.

The will is responsible for our view of the everyday world and for our vision of the point of leverage.

The technique of intention consists of precisely guiding the will.

To utter our intention in a loud voice is the secret of secrets.

Do it.

Search in unknown places.
Assume the responsibility of halting in face of the infinite.
There is no weakness in it.
It will not respond to prayers,
It will all fall down on you.
That does not matter.

This is like an angular stone, as if inscribed with certain precepts.

The universe is an infinite mass of energy fields.

They radiate from an unknown source, metaphorically called the Eagle.

Humankind is composed of such energy fields in the form of filaments. For the seer, who can perceive them, they are large luminous seeds, enmeshed in those filaments.

Of those threads, there is one group that shines intensely on the surface of the globe: that is where the assemblage point is. Castaneda used this term to describe a point of leverage, a fulcrum of energy, even of perception.

the assemblage point

Behind the luminous sphere of a human being, at the distance of an arm's length, there is a point of greater brilliance, the size of a tennis ball. An enormous number of energy fields pass through it, which appear as shining threads.

This site has important functions. One is that of perception, where energy is converted into sensory data. Another is the interpretation of such data into terms of everyday life. A sorcerer can displace this by means of a blow of the hand, struck between the shoulderblades, as Don Juan did with Castaneda many times.

Also, drugs can affect it, as well as a fever, hunger or tiredness. These are conditions that can displace the assemblage point. In general, the chance to see extraordinary things in those conditions is wasted, because the assemblage point needs to return to normality, to the way things were. Therefore, new habits are very important, as are the effects of 'doing nothing', as a way of changing the inventory of things that the assemblage point. As the point is moved, another section of energy fields converges upon it. Then other worlds are perceived and interpreted.

Sorcery, with its rituals and practices, is of indirect importance.

It is not ritual in itself that is sought after. Rather, by way of ritual, it is possible for the first attention to abandon the rigid control under which it finds itself. Thus the assemblage point can be shifted into a position of advanced consciousness.

In all human beings the assemblage point is located as already described. That gives rise to an appropriate view of the world. Although, as it is shifted, it tends to return to its original position, along with its worldview. But, meanwhile, according to wherever its new location may be, the assemblage point will engage with new perceptions: strange worlds or yet other ways of seeing everyday things. The ancient sorcerers said that there are at least 600 different other worlds. Eventually, the effect of the movement of the assemblage point is accumulative, leading toward a final outcome.

This relates to the comprehension of human consciousness.

e assemblage point
ust be moved from
inside,
nd that calls for
comprehension.

human being is a
creature
that is making a
voyage of
consciousness,
only for a moment
yet not a broken
journey.

Without that
confidence
we have nothing!

The solidity of the world is not an illusion. But it is indeed the stability of a point in a single place: that is to say, where there is a single description of the world.

> Common sense tricks us, because ordinary perception
> accounts for only one part
> of the truth ... not all of it.
> There has to be something more
> than our merely passing across the face of the Earth,
> allowing us only to eat and reproduce.

> If you examine for yourselves the social order,
> you will see that it is going nowhere.
> By completely taking stock of that order,
> we see that it has neither sense, nor direction, nor purpose.
> Do we think that money
> or other such things are of value?
> Or is it the biological imperative?

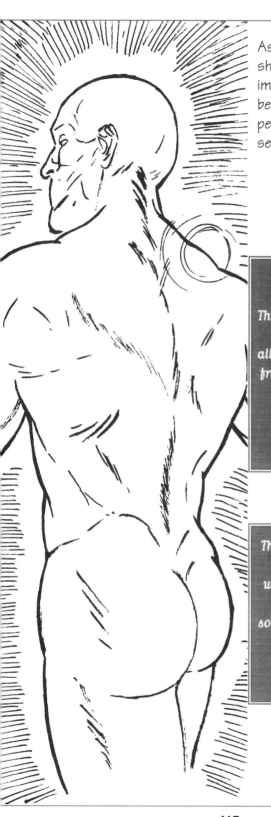

As the assemblage point is shifted, other energy fields immediately light up, so they can be perceived. The art of perceiving in this way is known as seeing.

The new position of the assemblage point
allows a world completely different from the everyday to be perceived: just as objective, just as real as the world we normally see.

The sorcerers enter into that other world
with the aim of obtaining energy, power,
solutions to general and particular problems —
or else to be confronted by the unimaginable.

The sorcerers were divided into two complementary bands, in accordance with their basic temperaments: the teachers of dreaming, those who participated in dreams; then, the stalkers, the trappers, those skilled in the art of ambush.

• THE TEACHERS OF DREAMING have the ability to enter into states of advanced consciousness by means of controlling their dreams. With training and development, they could convert that ability into the art of shared dreaming. This would enable them to shift, at will, the assemblage point from its habitual position.

• THE STALKERS possess the native skill to deal with deeds. With practice, a sorcerer transforms that capacity into the art of stalking. This consists of voluntarily maintaining the assemblage point fixed in the position where it has been relocated.

All those integrated into the group taught by Don Juan had an all round knowledge of both arts, but they would each be assigned to only one of the two bands.

Florinda Donner-Grau was a great teacher of dreaming. She was the author of three books: Shabono, The Dream of the Sorceress and Being in Dreaming.

stalking

This describes a group of procedures and attitudes that allow the best to be extracted from whatever determinate situation.

The stalkers can enter into states of advanced consciousness by using the control and management of their own behaviour. Stalking is the control of conduct.

For the stalkers, the management of controlled joking is fundamental. That is because they confront the tidal wave of everyday life, in the administration of commerce and dealing with people. From that position they can bend the will of whomsoever they like and get away with it.

Taisha Abelar was a distinguished stalker. She was the author of a book about sorcery, with the Spanish title of Donde cruzan los brujos.

principles

The art of stalking lists several principles.

1. A warrior goes to war only when he knows everything about a field of battle.
2. Everything that is unnecessary has to be eliminated.
3. Maximum concentration is called for to decide whether or not to go into battle. Every battle is a matter of life or death.
4. The warrior rests, forgets himself, and is afraid of nothing. Only then will the powers help him.
5. When faced with a superior form that cannot be engaged, the warrior withdraws for a while, and occupies himself with other things.
6. He strives to triumph. Therefore he compresses time, without squandering an instant.
7. He never shows his hand, and leaves himself open to nothing.

The shamans suggested applying these principles to everyday activities, beginning with small things and then arriving at life's major questions.

precepts

As opposed to most people, the warriors do not deal with the world so that the world may protect them. Instead, they count on the stalkers' rule, which contains three precepts.

1. Everything around us is an unfathomable mystery.
2. We should try to decipher mysteries, with no expectation of being able to do so.
3. The warrior considers himself to be a mystery. The mystery of being is infinite, whether that being is a stone, an ant or oneself. That is the humility that the warrior has. It means one is equal to everything.

The stalkers' rule can be applied to anything.

the three results

Following the seven principles in detail, one can observe everything without being at the focal point. Because of this, conflicts can be avoided or resolved.

1. The first result of applying those principles is that the stalkers learn to laugh at themselves. Since they are not afraid to take the role of the clown, they can make light of anything.
2. The second result is that they learn to have endless patience. They never make haste and are never irritated.
3. The third is that they come to develop an infinite capacity for improvisation.

In dreams, the assemblage point moves slightly, and it loses the stability it has in a normal state. Thus many emanations that are otherwise never used begin to shine.

To perfect the control of this natural movement is the art of managing the dreaming body.

Teachers of dreaming, those who participate in dreams, do not interfere with them, although the movement of the assemblage point does conform to the order of dreams.

How do they do it

You know that already — it comes with practice.

The exercises — such as looking at one's hands — are used to maintain stability in the new assemblage point, which is known as the dreaming position.

The art of stalking has allowed the shamans to fix the new point for sufficient time, so as to be witnesses of other worlds.

the double

Also known as 'the other', 'the energetic body' and 'the dreaming body', because it is a perfect replica of the dreamer.

It is concerned with the luminous being's own energy. This emanation is of a whitish colour.

In the second concentration, a human being tends to be focused in its entirety, as an energy field. Due to the stability of this concentration, a three dimensional image of the body is projected.

The double is not an apparition. It is as real as anything else we encounter in this world.

According to Don Juan, the interaction between both bodies results in an interpretation which is neither good nor bad, neither correct nor incorrect. It is an indivisible unity, which is of value to those journeying to the infinite.

As the two bodies come together, the miracle of freedom occurs. There is an awareness of beginning again a journey, interrupted at some point, into expanded consciousness. Therefore the shamans have said that perception has to be intended in its entirety.

The ancient seers belonged to a time cycle much earlier than the arrival of the Spaniards in Mexico. Those shamans were living between 7,000 and 10,000 years before that. Those figures contradict the schemes of classification used by academics of our own time.

They were powerful sorcerers, who unravelled mysteries and developed their knowledge ... true masters of the consciousness of being and of the art of dreaming. Frequently they used their capacities in a capricious way, so as to travel to other worlds. With the forces they could dispose of, they were very concrete, substantial figures of great usefulness.

They were invaded by conquerors from other Mesoamerican nations, who appropriated the entire Toltec world. Those invaders never learned to see, because they lacked the interior knowledge necessary to the task.

> When the Spanish conquistadors came, the ancient seers had already disappeared centuries before.

When the Spanish conquistadors came, the ancient seers had already disappeared centuries before.

The most important aspects of Toltec knowledge have been transmitted and have come down to us in near perfect condition. Particularly silent knowledge, a facet of the tradition that embraces the following themes:

- **magical passes;**
- **recapitulation;**
- **the centre of decisions;**
- **participation in dreams;**
- **interior silence.**

the new seers

They were and are the ones who survived the destruction of the earliest Toltec world. They were reclusive and undertook a new account of their practices. They confirmed the importance of stalking and ambush, participating in dreams, and intention.

The new time cycle began to establish itself at the time of the Spanish conquest. At that time there were many seers. During the colonial period their number was reduced gradually to a handful. The rest were exterminated. But the new seers were better prepared to face the danger. They mastered the art of ambush. So they were left alone and so they could explore further and give shape to their work.

The oppression they had to suffer under colonialism was a stimulus to refine

Everything is in order!

their new principles. Today there are only a few seers left. They have been dispersed everywhere.

They began a series of lineages, all at the same time and in the same manner. Toward the end of the 17th century, every nagual became enclosed within himself, confined to his own group, so as not to have direct contact with other seers. From that base, individual lineages were founded.

The early lineage of Don Juan and Castaneda was composed, counting from the 17th century, of 14 naguals, together with the groups formed around another number of seers.

In all there have been 27 naguals.

Since 1723, the appearance of another group of surrogates affected the eight naguals who followed, creating another line than that of the six naguals who had existed before that date.

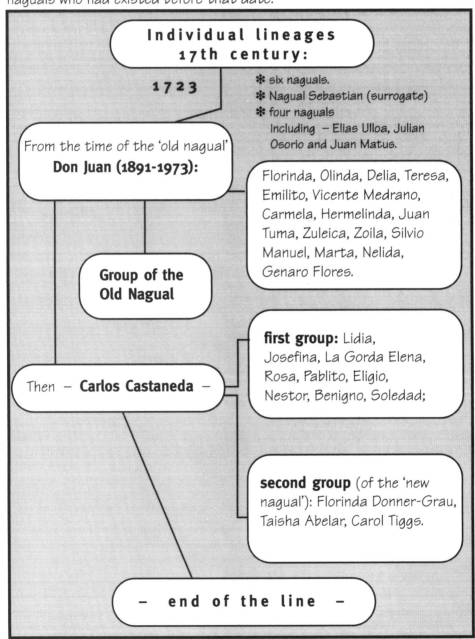

Individual lineages 17th century:

1723

✻ six naguals.
✻ Nagual Sebastian (surrogate)
✻ four naguals
  including – Elias Ulloa, Julian Osorio and Juan Matus.

From the time of the 'old nagual'
Don Juan (1891-1973):

Florinda, Olinda, Delia, Teresa, Emilito, Vicente Medrano, Carmela, Hermelinda, Juan Tuma, Zuleica, Zoila, Silvio Manuel, Marta, Nelida, Genaro Flores.

Group of the Old Nagual

first group: Lidia, Josefina, La Gorda Elena, Rosa, Pablito, Eligio, Nestor, Benigno, Soledad;

Then – **Carlos Castaneda** –

second group (of the 'new nagual'): Florinda Donner-Grau, Taisha Abelar, Carol Tiggs.

– end of the line –

Castaneda died in the Spring of 1998, but the news of his death was not released until the Summer.

At the turn of the 80s and 90s, Castaneda remained a mythical figure.

His books had appeared at regular intervals. In them, Don Juan and Don Genaro are still present, among other sorcerers. Castaneda kept his narratives in chronological order. As his experiences occurred at a different level of advanced perception, the method of recounting them required effort and time for reflection. This enabled him to give an account of new teachings.

> In a universe forced to change, is there any written word that does not change also?
> That would be the world of the taxidermist.
> I am not writing fiction ...
> I tell things as they happen ...

> The belief system that I came to study has devoured me ...

Castaneda's books are largely above the category of best sellers and they are translated into almost all other languages. Year upon year, new generations of readers join the legion of his loyal followers. He became, as earlier in his life, the subject of publishers' hype. There were many versions of the things said about him: that he went about barefoot, like Jesus; that he was under the influence of drugs all day; that he had killed himself — he was said to have died in several different places.

While Don Juan was alive, Castaneda had made various journeys. He decided to turn his back on the world. When the sorcerer passed away, he travelled to Europe, mainly to Spain and Italy.

Europe is dead ...
It lacks the strength and the thrust
of which there is so much
on the American continent.

For three years, Castaneda lived in Guatemala. After that he was living at one place in Mexico and at another in Los Angeles. He travelled about in a dormobile. He paid for everything with a credit card. He practised kung fu every day.

I struggle against getting old e you can't imagine.

If we are going to die altogether, completely, why not live life in the same way?

159

With Castaneda and his three women companions, the lineage of sorcerers around Don Juan came to an end. The special configuration of energy among the four of them made it impossible to carry on the line.

In face of this ending, Castaneda and the rest of the group shared in an idea put forward by Carol Tiggs.

To explain the world that Don Juan gave us to inherit is our final expression of gratitude to him. Our purpose is to continue searching for what he was searching for: liberty.

Don Juan was not interested just in teaching alone, rather in the perpetuation of his lineage.

That not being possible, the group decided to end with a gold seal: passing on their knowledge of magical passes, maintained until now in their secret ritual.

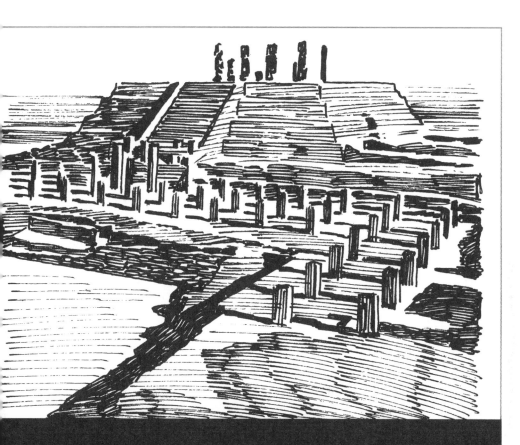

The group focused principally on California and Mexico for the public dissemination of its teachings.

Characteristic of this stage was the setting up of workshops and seminars, sometimes in other parts of the US and also in Europe.

The assistants in these enterprises include three women: Kyle Lundahl, Reni Murez and Nyei Murez, who were known as 'chacmools'. This name comes from the large sculpted human figures found among the pyramids of Tula — the ancient capital of the Toltecs — on the Yucatan peninsula of Mexico.

To Don Juan the chacmools represented the warrior guardians of the pyramids, as seats of power.

These women spent their daily lives in magical passes. They taught their knowledge in the seminars given by Tensegrity until December 1995.

Another group of warrior guardians replaced those women. At first they were called explorers, in the belief that they would discover new pathways and solutions. Later they were called energy trackers, because their task was to follow the scant trace that energy left behind as it flowed away. They were channellers of energy, with the particular ability not to impose their own will. All they were after was that energy should show itself to them. They also taught at Tensegrity seminars.

The appearance of The Blue Explorer (who would participate in seminars) was foretold by Don Juan.

Meetings were led by Florinda, Taisha, Carol and Castaneda, although he did not always appear personally. This fuelled rumours about him.

If not, everything would have been turned into something else ...

business

Castaneda had business relations with three corporations. He explained this by saying that to disseminate his teachings in the modern world required media resources that he and his group did not, as individuals, have.

Castaneda set up a website on the Internet.

He produced several publications under the imprint of Voyagers to the Infinite, which was also a review of applied hermeneutics, bringing together Western philosophical speculation and the observations and findings of the ancient shamans.

He made sure that the interests of those corporations would not become predominant and that they would remain in line with the ideas of Don Juan.

philosophy

The term intentionality has its origin among the medieval schoolmen.

Also it is related to the ideas of the philosopher Franz Brentano (1838-1917), who with his descriptive psychology is regarded as the father of the phenomenological school. For Brentano, mental phenomena have the property of retaining and referring to objects that do not exist. Thus, only mental phenomena alone can include intentionality. Brentano maintained that since no physical phenomenon can be in itself intentional, whatever is termed mental cannot stem from the brain.

Castaneda added that intention, for the shamans, transcends the known world. It is a wave of energy, a beam that is confined to itself, adhering to itself.

The German mathematician and philosopher Edmund Gustav Husserl (1859-1938) was the first in the West to conceive of the possibility of 'suspending judgment'. Phenomenological method puts in parentheses those elements that sustain ordinary perception. Phenomenology is a descriptive philosophy of experience, according to which the act of knowing, of knowledge, depends on intention and not on perception.

Don Juan transcended the level of theory and went further than the suspension of judgment: he dismantled the perceptive prejudgments that Castaneda had, to the extent that they had to be totally abandoned.

For some of us, there are themes proper to philosophical discipline that can be linked to the discipline of the shamans.

DON JUAN MATUS

E.G. HUSSERL

from magical passes...

The physical body embraces both the body and the mind.

And it is balanced, as a unity, against the energetic body.

Millennia before the Spanish conquest, shamans of ancient Mexico had discovered a series of bodily movements which had given them such physical and mental wellbeing that they decided to call them magical passes. Those sorcerers were able to advance their consciousness by using those passes, thus realising incredible perceptive achievements.

Magical passes were taught from generation to generation among practising shamans, using complex rituals and including major secrets.

Those skills were transmitted to Don Juan and so to Castaneda and his fellow travellers. They were the most functional features of his teaching.

...to tensegrity

Castaneda's principal activity, in the company of the sorceresses, came to be the dissemination of a discipline of physical exercises under the name of Tensegrity. Their seminars devoted several hours to instruction in these exercises, which were considered to be at the heart of the way of the warrior.

Tensegrity developed out of modifying the magical passes from movements that were entirely personal to each of Don Juan's four disciples into movements that could generally be applicable to anybody.

The word Tensegrity comes from architecture and, by extension, signifies a synthesis of tension and integration, expressions which denote the two impulsive forces of the magical passes. There are many movements, grouped into six series:

- for the preparation of intention;
- for the womb;
- the five interests series (Westwood series);
- the heat series (for separating right and left hand bodies);
- the masculinity series;
- a series of devices, combined with specific magical passes.

The movements lead to showing how excessive preoccupation with the ego can generate fatigue. Also they produce enough energy to ensure that such preoccupations can be abandoned — something which cannot be done intellectually.

The practices of Tensegrity, either individually or collectively, make it possible to redistribute energy and its three effects: disconnection of interior dialogue; achieving interior silence; flexibility of the assemblage point.

With Tensegrity's method, conserving energy is facilitated, as is the cohesion of the energetic body. Consequently, physical wellbeing is promoted. In reality, energy neither enters nor leaves a human being, given that the body is itself a mass of energy. Due to redistribution, energy is relocated at the vital centres, giving the sensation that energy is increased.

One magical aspect of the movements prescribed by Tensegrity is the chance to connect with the spirit, establishing a link with the life force. Also a similar consciousness can be reached by following the precepts of the warrior. It is the awareness that there is an agglutinative force, which vibrates and gives cohesion to the energetic body.

When hundreds of people follow these practices together, an energetic current takes shape amongst them. That is one of the effects of the human mass. This generates a sense of urgency, felt as a vibrating wind which can confer on people the primary elements of Tensegrity's purpose.

It's not merely a matter of exercises.
It's a way to summon up power.

If the practices are followed by an even larger group, the changes will be greater
...
and unforeseeable.

Castaneda is no longer with us – the man who made his own the proposition of not fulfilling agreements in the formulation of which he did not participate. He died on April 27, 1998. Mystery was upheld once again: the news did not come out until some time later. His body was cremated without ceremony and the ashes were taken to Mexico.

People have a profound sense of magic, but the need to be rational is a barrier. The everyday world is so powerful that it allows us no exit. We are taught from very early on to be obsessed with the social person and not the total person. The years that are spent in this way eradicate magic. One can exist only in the ego and such stupidness. Don Juan, with his teachings, could open the way for a much more interesting kind of human being: someone who could live already in a magical world or universe.

Some terms are omitted, because they are already explained in the text. Other words appear here and in the text as well. Also, expressions from Castaneda's own books and publications are included. Most of these follow Castaneda's own personal use of English terms, in a way which is loose enough for similar words to be expressed in a similar way. Freedom seems to be of the essence here.

A & B FORCES: a characteristic duality in the universe and amongst humankind. the A Force is used in everyday action and activity. It is represented by a straight vertical line. The B Force is rarely active and remains in darkness. It is represented by a horizontal line.

ABSTRACT: the spirit, which needs to be known by no words or thoughts. The quest for freedom.

ATTENTION or CONCENTRATION, ON DREAMING: specific to the art of dreaming, participation in dreams and conjuring the stuff of dreams.

BLUE EXPLORER: a particular entity belonging to the world of inorganic beings.

THE BORDER, or FRONTIER, OF HUMANKIND: the limit of a human being's capacity for perception.

CHALLENGERS OF DEATH: ancient seers who used the technique of burying themselves for very long periods.

CONCRETE, MONUMENTAL, SUBSTANTIAL: the practical part of sorcery and its techniques.

CONTROL: refining the spirit in face of maltreatment.

CONTROLLED FOLLY: the art of pretending to be immersed in action, seeming genuinely to be seen to separate oneself from everything, without ceasing to be an integral part of it.

DISCIPLINE: the skill of confronting serenely those difficulties that do not figure in our expectations.

The **EAGLE:** also known as the dark sea of consciousness. The power that governs the destiny of all living things.

The **EMISSARY OF DREAMS:** energy that assumes the teaching and support of explorers, reminding them of things they already know.

ENERGETIC BODY: the counterpart of the physical body. A sphere made of pure energy which sees and displaces itself, vanishing.

ENERGY (stretching through the sinews and tendons): a vital current that moves at the deepest level of the body's musculature, from the neck to the fingers and toes.

EXPLORERS (INORGANIC BEINGS): energy charges and forces that mix with the objects of real dreaming. They investigate consciousness. They are aggressive and dangerous and they come in various shapes and sizes.

GUARDIAN WARRIOR: someone whop accepts the responsibility of being a custodian.

IMPECCABILITY: that which makes for correctness in a determinate situation. To be free of fears and rational assumptions. The best use of personal energy.

INTENSITY: the effect of instant perception, in a state of advanced awareness.

INTENTION: the quiet activity of following spaces left empty by direct sensory perception. The act of enriching phenomena observable by means of intention.

LIFT OFF: an impulse growing from consciousness of the planet itself, as a living organism.

NAGUAL: one of the two aspects or counterparts that constitute the equal of humankind. It is something beyond the reach of most men and women, beyond description. However, it is something which can be witnessed. The word also refers to the leader, which guides other sources. The nagual also has extraordinary qualities and and exceptional energetic configuration. See tonal.

NAGUAL WOMAN: the feminine counterpart of nagual energy. She accompanies the nagual of the group that preceded her in the shift of the world of perceptions. The exception is Carol Tiggs, whose group brought the lineage of Don Juan to a close.

NOT DOING, DOING NOTHING: that which is excluded from everything that may be known. A cognitive process to interrupt, deliberately, the flow of an activity. Also, to check the momentary chaos resulting from the acquisition of mobility in thought and action.

ORGANIC BEINGS: unusually luminous beings, round in shape. The effect rapid movements. Their lives and consciousness are short.

PERCEIVING: of special interest to the shaman. It consists of interpretation of the direct flow of energy, with no influence of the mind.

PERSONAL IMPORTANCE: strength generated by self image, maintaining the assemblage point in present time. The intention should be to sublimate and suppress it.

POWER PLANTS: three hallucinogenic pants — Lopophora Williamsii, Datura inoxia and Psylobice mexicana. They are used to shift the assemblage point and to expand consciousness. It is extremely dangerous to use these products except in very carefully controlled circumstances. The effects can be so dangerous as to lead to instant death.

RECAPITULATION: systematic vision and revision of the experiences of one's own life. This multiplies the possibilities of freeing oneself from self reflection.

REDISTRIBUTION OF ENERGY: The process of transporting, from one place to another, the energy that already exists within ourselves.

REMEMBERING: keeping track of the assemblage point, in the position where it was when certain events took place.

SATURATION: bombardment of the body with masses of magical passes. This allows for guidance of the strength that gives a person unity. It creates the maximum overall effect.

SILENT KNOWLEDGE: The act of making ourselves conscious of our link with intention.

SKIMMING: when perceiving emanations, choosing the best of everything.

SORCERER: a person with knowledge, who is acquainted with cosmic energy and utilises it precisely.

STALKERS: inorganic beings who follow the spaces left by consciousness of being.

STOPPING THE WORLD: an interruption of the interpretation of an altered state of consciousness, enabling things to be seen in a different way.

SURROGATE: an ancient seer who received energy from the new naguals, in exchange for favours and certain knowledge known as 'gifts of power'.

SYNTACTICAL COMMANDS or CONTROLS: Formulas, even clichés, used for praise or detrimental remarks, incorporated into the language, which may govern human behaviour. The sorcerers avoid them.

TALES OF SORCERY: stories about the nagual, which crop up at particular moments during apprenticeship. Such stories are designed to make abstract things comprehensible.

TONAL: the opposite of every living thing. It constitutes everything that may be known in this world, including ourselves. Its purpose is protective, because it organises the chaos of the world. See nagual.

The WAY OF THE WARRIOR: the code of conduct characterised by impeccable action.

The WILL: that which channels the energy of any living thing, to produce whatever may lie within the limits of possibility.

the authors

Martín Broussalis: Born in Buenos Aires, he is the author of a book of short stories *Resurrección de los muertos*, two novels *Al Divino botón* and *Basada en un caso real* and a comedy *Super 8 volante*. The novels and the play were written in collaboration with Diego Recalde. Broussalis is editor and publisher of the review *Guyana Comic*. He has also written for the newspaper *Renacer* and has adapted a novel by the French writer Octave Mirbeau as a comic strip.

Martín Arvallo is an Argentinian artist. He has worked on animated films and is graphics editor of the review *Guyana Comic* and has worked for the newspaper *Renacer*. He illustrated *Al Divino botón* for Broussalis and Recalde and also made the drawings for *Krishnamurti for Beginners*™. Arvallo studies the violin.

index

A

Abelar, Taisha 134, 149, 156, 162
advanced consciousness
        123-4, 126, 139, 148-9
adversaries 129
allies 26
Art of Dreaming, The (Castaneda) 121
assemblage point 144-7, 148, 152, 167
attention on dreaming 72, 137-40, 169

B

Beat Generation 8
Beatles, The 6
being, conscious of 143
Being in Dreaming (Donner-Grau) 148
benefactors 90, 92
Berkeley, California 31
Big Sur and the Oranges
        of Hieronymus Bosch (Miller) 8
Blue Explorer 162, 169
Brentano, Franz 164
Burroughs, William 8

C

cacti 15
Castaneda, Carlos
    and business connections 163
    and cigarettes 58
    as Cordoba 115-20
    death of 157, 168
    and diet 59
    early life of 2
    education of 3-4, 10
    and Florinda 97, 113, 119
    and friendship 56
    and groups 130-1, 134-5
    as hunter 62-5
    legacy of 157-63, 168
    and marriage 4
    and mescalin 18-19
    and personal history 33, 52, 54
    and personal power 71
    and powerbase 17
    and relationships 57
    and routine breaking 54, 66
    and seeing 34-6, 40-1
    and shaman apprenticeship
        12-29, 34-45, 84-94
    and sleeping 55
    and state of separate reality 27-9, 45
    and tasks 115-20
    and teaching 157-61
    and Tensegrity 128, 161, 162, 166-7
    and toloache 21-3
    and travelling 158-9
    writing by 30, 32, 45, 48, 50, 75,
        121-2, 158
Castaneda, Carlton (son) 4
chacmools 161
Chicago, USA 31
children 103, 138
cigarettes 58
City College, Los Angeles 3
Cohn-Bendit, Daniel (Danny the Red) 30
concentration on dreaming 72,
        137-40, 169
confusion, controlling 37, 87
conjuring, art of 72
consciousness 122-4, 139
Cordoba, Joe (Castaneda) 115-20
Corso, Gregory 8
'cutting edge' 103

D

death 38-9
decisions, centre of (liquid centre) 128
Detroit, USA 31
diet 59
'doing nothing' 68, 139, 144, 170
Don Genaro Flores:
        as benefactor to Castaneda 90

and Castaneda's apprenticeship
40-1, 46-7, 76-7, 79, 93
and last time sees Castaneda 94
Don Juan Matus:
first meets Castaneda 10-11
and Castaneda's apprenticeship
12-19, 34-48, 84-94
passes over 122
in a suit 84-5
Donde cruzan los brujos (Abelar) 149
Donner-Grau, Florinda (Gina) 134, 135,
148, 156, 162
Doors of Perception, The (Huxley) 8
'double', the 153
Dream of the Sorceress, The
(Donner-Grau) 148
dreams 72-3, 139, 148, 152-3
drugs 7, 15, 144

E

Eagle, The 107-10, 140, 143, 169
Eagle's Gift, The (Castaneda) 121
egoism 101, 114
Elena (apprentice) 113, 115, 118, 120
energy 80-1, 143, 144, 147, 162, 169
energy trackers (explorers) 162
explanations 133

F

Ferlinghetti, Lawrence 8
fighting stance (dance) 28
Florinda (teacher) 97, 113, 119, 134
Flower Power movement 5-9
flying 25
France 30
free will 43
friendships 56

G

games (Toltec) 68
Gandi, Mahatma 129
Garfinkel, Harold 30
Ginsburg, Allen 8
groups (apprentices) 134-5

H

hallucinations 15, 18-19
Heaven and Hell (Huxley) 8
herbs 15
Hippies 5, 8-9
hongo (Psylobice mexicana) 15
Howl (Ginsburg) 8
human pattern 99-100
hunters 62-6
Husserl, Edmund Gustav 164
Huxley, Aldous 8

I

intellect 136
intentionality 141, 164, 170
interior dialogue 167
interior silence 44, 125, 126, 167
Interior Silence (Castaneda) 121
internal dialogue 73, 74

J

Journey to Ixtlán (Castaneda) 48, 50

K

Kabouter movement (Netherlands) 31
Kerouac, Jack 8
Kesey, Ken 8
King, Martin Luther 31
knowledge, shamanic 12, 14-16, 20, 106

L

leap forward (Shaman) 95
Leary, Dr Timothy 7
liquid centre, see decisions, centre of
Lord of the Rings (Tolkien) 8
love 101
luminous seed 80, 92-3, 142, 143
Lundahl, Kyle 161

M

magic 43, 48
magical passes 165
Magical Passes (Castaneda) 121
Meighan, Dr (ethnography tutor) 10
mescalin 17-19

Mescalito (spirit of mescalin) 19
Mexico 31
Miller, Henry 8
mitote (four day festival) 19
Murez, Nyei 161
Murey, Reni 161
mushrooms 15, 24, 26, 51

N

nagual:
    and attention (second kind) 139
    and benefactors 90
    and centre of the self 81
    definition of 88, 170
    and guides 127, 155-6
    and stages of passing 93-4
Naked Lunch, The (Burroughs) 8
National Enquirer 54
Nestor (apprentice) 90, 94, 96
Netherlands 31

O

On the Road (Kerouac) 8
One Flew over the Cuckoo's Nest (Kesey) 7

P

Pablito (apprentice) 90, 94, 96
pacifism 5, 129
parents 103
Paris Student movement (1968) 30
partir technique 90
Paz, Octavio 31
perception:
    and advanced consciousness 123
    and attention 137-8
    definition of 170
    and the Eagle 108
    and partir 90
    and readers of the infinite 125
    and warriors 106
    wings of 94
personal history 33, 52, 54
personal recapitulation (or appraisal) 109-11

peyote (Lopophora Williamsii)
    7, 10-11, 15, 16, 18-19
phenomenology 164
plants, psychotropic:
    as allies 26
    definition of 170
    and expansion of consciousness 51
    hongo 15
    peyote 7, 10-11, 15-19
    toloache 15, 21-3, 26
point of leverage 51, 110, 142, 143
power 21, 24, 69-71, 83-5
Power of Silence, The (Castaneda) 121
powerbase 17
pragmatism 132
Provo movement (Netherlands) 31

R

readers of the infinite 125
reading 54
reason (ring of power) 83
regular habits 54, 59, 66
relationships 57
Ryan, Margaret (wife) 4

S

San Francisco, USA 6
Sartre, Jean-Paul 30
'second concentration' 72
Second Ring of Power, The (Castaneda) 121
seeing, learning to 34-6, 40-1, 78, 80, 147
seers (new) 155-6
self, centre of the 81-2
self appraisal 109-11
self awareness, sense of 76
self importance 60
sensory interpretation 13
separate reality 27-9
Separate Reality, A (Castaneda) 45
sexual needs 101, 102
Shabono (Donner-Grau) 148
Shankar, Ravi 6
shamanism:

and advanced consciousness 123-4,
126, 139, 148-9
and allies 15-16, 26, 51, 60, 170
ancient 154-5, 165
and death 38-9
and dreams 72-3, 139, 148, 152-3
and the Eagle 107-10, 140, 143, 169
and flying 25
and hunters 62-3
and knowledge 12, 14-16, 20, 106
and the leap forward 95
new seers 155-6
and readers of the infinite 25
and seeing 34-6, 40-1, 78, 80, 147
and silent knowledge 126-7, 171
two bands of 148-51,
see also warriors (shaman)
silent knowledge 126-7, 171
sleeping 55
smoke (smokey) mushroom 24
solitude, state of 101
sorcery 106, see also shamanism
Spain 31
spirituality 132
stalkers 148-51, 171
'stopping the world' technique 50, 171
student protests (1960's) 30-1
survival 118
Szasz, Dr Thomas S. 7

T

Tales of Power (Castaneda) 75
tasks (Toltec) 111-12
Teachings of Don Juan-a Yaki Way of
Knowledge, The (Castaneda) 30, 32
Tensegrity 128, 161, 162, 166-7
Terry (helper) 116-17
Tiggs, Carol 134, 156, 160, 162
toloache (Datura inoxia) 15, 21-3, 26
Tolkien, J. R. R. 8
Toltec traditions 68, 72, 104-9, 154
tonal 81, 87, 88, 89, 92, 93, 94, 171

'Tropics' novels (Miller) 8

U

United States of America 4-8, 31

W

warriors (shaman):
and attention (third kind) 140
code of conduct 171
in control 57
and the Eagle 108
free from form 100
and free will 42
guardians 161-2
and human beings 85
and mystery of the world 44, 86
and perceiving energy 35
and personal power 69-70
Propositions 106
and self awareness 76
and stalking 150-1
Watts, Alan 8
way forward 67
Way of Zen (Watts) 8
will (ring of power) 83, 142, 171
worries 65
women 97-8, 170

Z

Zappa, Frank 6

How to get original thinkers to come to your home...

ADDICTION & RECOVERY (£7.99)
ADLER (£7.99)
AFRICAN HISTORY (£7.99)
ARABS & ISRAEL (£7.99)
ARCHITECTURE (£7.99)
BABIES (£7.99)
BENJAMIN (£7.99)
BIOLOGY (£7.99)
BLACK HISTORY (£7.99)
BLACK HOLOCAUST (£7.99)
BLACK PANTHERS (£7.99)
BLACK WOMEN (£7.99)
BODY (£7.99)
BRECHT (£7.99)
BUDDHA (£7.99)
CASATNEDA (£7.99)
CHE (£7.99)
CHOMSKY (£7.99)
CLASSICAL MUSIC (£7.99)
COMPUTERS (£7.99)
THE HISTORY OF CINEMA (£9.99)
DERRIDA (£7.99)
DNA (£7.99)
DOMESTIC VIOLENCE (£7.99)
THE HISTORY OF EASTERN EUROPE (£7.99)
ELVIS (£7.99)
ENGLISH LANGUAGE (£7.99)
EROTICA (£7.99)
FANON (£7.99)
FOOD (£7.99)
FOUCAULT (£7.99)
FREUD (£7.99)
GESTALT (£7.99)
HEALTH CARE (£7.99)
HEIDEGGER (£7.99)
HEMINGWAY (£7.99)
ISLAM (£7.99)

HISTORY OF CLOWNS (£7.99)
I CHING (£7.99)
JAZZ (£7.99)
JEWISH HOLOCAUST (£7.99)
JUDAISM (£7.99)
JUNG (£7.99)
KIERKEGAARD (£7.99)
KRISHNAMURTI (£7.99)
LACAN (£7.99)
MALCOLM X (£7.99)
MAO (£7.99)
MARILYN (£7.99)
MARTIAL ARTS (£7.99)
MCLUHAN (£7.99)
MILES DAVIS (£7.99)
NIETZSCHE (£7.99)
OPERA (£7.99)
PAN-AFRICANISM (£7.99)
PHILOSOPHY (£7.99)
PLATO (£7.99)
POSTMODERNISM (£7.99)
STRUCTURALISM&
POSTSTRUCTURALISM (£7.99)
PSYCHIATRY (£7.99)
RAINFORESTS (£7.99)
SAI BABA (£7.99)
SARTRE (£7.99)
SAUSSURE (£7.99)
SCOTLAND (£7.99)
SEX (£7.99)
SHAKESPEARE (£7.99)
STANISLAVSKI (£7.99)
UNICEF (£7.99)
UNITED NATIONS (£7.99)
US CONSTITUTION (£7.99)
WORLD WAR II (£7.99)
ZEN (£7.99)